In *What Daddy Did*, Donna Ford – author of the bestselling book, *The Step Child* – tells the rest of her story. While it is a tale of the appalling physical, mental and emotional inheritance left to Donna, it is also a tale of how exhilaration, tenderness and self-development can flourish despite childhood horrors. *What Daddy Did* will speak to readers of how we all can find hope from the darkest of histories. Visit Donna's website www.donnamford.com.

WHAT
DADDY
DID

The shocking true story of a little girl betrayed

Donna Ford

1 3 5 7 9 10 8 6 4 2

Published in 2008 by Vermilion, an imprint of Ebury Publishing
This edition published by Vermilion in 2009

Ebury Publishing is a Random House Group company

The Random House Group Limited Reg. No. 954009

Addresses for companies within the Random House Group can be found at
www.rbooks.co.uk

A CIP catalogue record for this book is available from the British Library

Penguin Random House is committed to a sustainable future for
our business, our readers and our planet. This book is made from
Forest Stewardship Council® certified paper.

Printed and bound in Great Britain by Clays Ltd, Elcograf S.p.A.

ISBN 9780091924034

Copies are available at special rates for bulk orders. Contact the sales
development team on 020 7840 8487 for more information.

To buy books by your favourite authors and register for offers, visit
www.rbooks.co.uk

I'd like to dedicate this book to the memory of Auntie Nellie, Bob, Flora and Dan the man – gone but never ever forgotten.

With love, Donna xx

᠄

CONTENTS

$\sim$

ACKNOWLEDGEMENTS

To Linda Watson-Brown, an extremely talented writer who has worked with me on both of my books, gently prodding me and pushing me to clarify my thoughts while supporting me as only a true friend can do. Linda, I thank you for your love and skill, for holding me when I was breaking my heart, for making me feel so safe by cuddling me up in furry blankets and letting me weep while our children all slept safely upstairs.

To Jenny Brown, my agent – your friendship I value, your talent and professionalism I am in awe of. Thank you, Jenny – I love both you and Linda so much because you are also wonderful mothers.

To Clare Hulton at Random House – thank you for believing in me, for listening to my story and for the respect you show me. To Julia Kellaway, who came in to the story halfway, but has contributed so much in the way of making this project as smooth-running as possible, and to Roger Field, who has dealt with the legal readings both sensitively and professionally. Thank you all so much – these books wouldn't have been possible without you all.

Thank you to Paul, Claire, Saoirse, Hannah, Katy, Andrea,

Tony, Fiona, Derek and Matthew for being the best family EVER! I love you all.

And thank you to Christine and Stuart – your unconditional love has been at times overwhelming, your friendship astounding. You are the most wonderful people I have ever had the pleasure to meet.

To Saritha, Tim and Shalini – it will never matter which continent divides us; friendship has no boundaries. I love you all.

To Elaine – well, they did call it puppy love!

And last, but by no means least, to my little sister Karen. Thank you for showing me, when no-one else could, that it was possible to give and receive love. I love you and a special kiss and hug for Claire and Hannah, love Auntie Donna xxx

PROLOGUE

PROLOGUE

Edinburgh, 2007

My name is Donna Ford.
I am 48 years old.
I used to be a really, really, really bad little girl.
Now I am a really, really, really good mother.

I'M NOT BAD any more. I never was. My stepmother was the evil one, but since trying to face what she did to me as a child – what she *allowed* to be done to me – I have tried to focus on the good things in my life.

And there are lots.

My pride and joy, my wonders, are my three children. I have just come back from a holiday in Greece with my eldest daughter, Claire, and it was a fantastic experience. Now that I'm home, my youngest child, Saoirse, is in my arms, telling me her news, and hugging me as if she'll never let me go. I look over to my telephone and see the answering machine blinking. I get up, walk over and casually press the button to hear who has been trying to get me. It's my son, Paul. He wants to tell me that he and his fiancée have got their first flat together. The excitement is flooding from his voice. He sounds as if all of his Christmases have come at once! Saoirse and Claire pick up on the atmosphere and start dancing in the living room. They know how much this means to Paul and they are delighted for him.

And me?

The room starts spinning.

There's a buzzing noise in my ears.

I feel hot and cold all at once.

I think I'm going to faint – no, I think I'm going to scream.

Will anyone see me if I do? Will anyone hear me if I do?

I turn round to the girls and tell them how wonderful everything is. The words don't stick in my throat, but they stick in my heart.

I'm going to have to go back.

⁓

Before I went on holiday with Claire, Paul had told me that he was looking at flats with his fiancée. As with most cities, there are only so many places young people can afford to rent in Edinburgh when they are taking their first steps to independence. Older areas. Areas which used to be predominantly working class. Areas with tenements and flats and a dirty grey feel to them that no amount of rejuvenation schemes and Lottery money will ever take away. Places just like the one in which I was raised.

My father, Don, and my stepmother, Helen, had taken me from my Barnardo's home when I was four years old and brought me to Easter Road. In that flat, Helen practised her abuse of me. It was there that she would beat me and flail me and scream at me and lock me up and starve me. It was there that she would tell me I was evil, that I was ugly, that I was a bastard, that no good would ever come to me because a little girl like me didn't deserve good things in her life.

When we all lived in that flat, I thought it couldn't get worse. I should have known.

We moved to a new house in Edina Place, a street just off Easter Road, where Helen could perfect her skills. She kept on with her campaign of hatred, but she also decided to bring in some additional help. Physically and verbally abusing me just wasn't enough for her – not when she could have her special 'parties'. Parties where she would invite men to do whatever they wanted with me, and where she could act the convivial hostess. Parties where she would stand outside my bedroom door as I was raped. In Edina Place, I grew to dread the sound of the doorbell, the particular rings which the men would use.

Even when I was an adult, and Helen had finally been found guilty in a court of law, I still avoided that area at all costs. When I visited my sister-in-law who lived, and still lives, at Leith Links, I would drive a long, convoluted way round just to avoid the area where there were so many bad memories. I knew before I went on holiday that Paul was looking at a flat in Edina Place. When he told me I shuddered but thought no more about it. I reasoned there was no point in getting myself worried unless it actually happened.

And it has.

Paul calls for me a few days after my return from Greece. He has been desperate to show me the flat he has managed to find. Thankfully, he is blissfully unaware of my fears and is caught up in the excitement of his new life unfolding before him – while I dread facing my past. We are driving up Easter Road and Paul is chatting incessantly about all his news; his beautiful fiancée, Ayumi; his walking trip in the Pyrenees; his trip next year to Japan; all his hopes for the future. I smile and laugh and encourage him, but inside I feel a ball of anxiety winding itself into a tighter and tighter knot. I am genuinely petrified at the thought of visiting a flat in this street, of being back here again.

When we arrive at Edina Place we manage to find a parking space, eventually, in front of what was once a printing shop and is now housing. We get out of the car and Paul leads me in the direction of my childhood home. But we aren't going there, I tell myself, we're going to his home. It might not be too close; it might not bring back anything to me.

Number 31 is a main door flat and Paul's flat is in the next-door tenement block on the top floor. As we approach the steps, my anxiety is getting worse. I can hear a murmuring noise getting louder and louder. The echoes from my past are gathering in force. Not much has changed about this area and I try to focus on superficial things: the number of cars that make it so busy; the dinginess of the Co-op building; the new housing that has sprung up in every nook and cranny.

As we approach number 31, I see that all that has changed here is the colour of the front door, from maroon to white. I am still filled with dread. I can hear Paul chatting excitedly and I know that I am answering him but, at the same time, I am being transported right back into my past. I look at the old house and half expect my father to come stumbling out of the door or for Helen to roar another order for me to 'get in here now, you little bitch!'

I manage to keep walking, with the voices getting louder, the past getting closer, until we get to the door of Paul's building. When we actually enter the stairway, I think that I'm going to vomit. I turn to Paul and, before I can explain anything, he says, 'Oh, Mum! Let's go and check out the garden – it's lovely!'

❧

After my first book was published, I deliberately came back to Edinburgh to face my demons and see everything in a different light. I genuinely love this city, but I want it to disappear at this moment. Paul isn't being insensitive – he, like his sisters, doesn't know the extent of the abuse I suffered as a child. He has a copy of my book and will choose to read it at some point in his life, or maybe never. It doesn't matter – all that matters is that he does what he wants, that he follows his own choices. I know why my two older children haven't read it yet. Claire told me that I was their hero, their rock, and that they didn't want to think of me as vulnerable when I had always been so strong for them. I have been very happy for this to be the way, but it does mean that Paul is blissfully oblivious of my fears here today.

I am glad about that because this is his moment. However, as we start to descend the stairs to the basement (the only way to get out to the garden), I wish that I could be a million miles away. The stairway is just as I always remember, identical to the one in my childhood 'home'. There is the same worn stone staircase and, what seems to me, the same paintwork and the same smell. The smell! A horrible, damp stench – the stink of mixed living.

It is so, so dark and I'm beginning to tremble. I know that I'm going back there. I have to keep dragging myself into the present because the strength of the flashback I'm having is so strong. I follow Paul down the stairs to the basement, which is also still the same as I remember. The steps lead down to a corridor going left to what would have been the coal store, and the right side leads to the garden. I am following my son with real trepidation and I'm visibly trembling. Paul looks back at me and asks if I'm all right because he can see me shaking. I pull myself together and push back what has just forced its way into my mind. A memory that has hit me like a sledgehammer.

I follow Paul out into the back garden. I get immediate joy and comfort from the sun. To my surprise, it is so lovely out here, and that is what I will focus on. There is a beautiful, cultivated lawn with a herbaceous border, all lovingly tended by a man who is tidying and pruning. Paul introduces himself to this neighbour, which gives me a chance to really look around. All of these back greens adjoin the rear of the tenement blocks and I feel compelled to walk into what was once ours. I walk over and look up at the old kitchen window and down at the old cellar where I took many a beating.

The flashback I've had is still shouting at me to let it through, but what I can see now is that this is a different place. Those people who hurt me are long gone and I am the only one who can let them through again. I can take this experience and make it a positive one. Paul's house will be filled with laughter and love. I will visit him there and I will make sure I do it with joy in my heart.

I can do this.

I can.

So, why do I still feel a chill on my heart and hear the ghosts in my head?

༜

Chapter One

My Past, My Present, My Future

I'M A DIFFERENT WOMAN to the one I was in the winter of 2001 when the police knocked at my door. They were there to inform me that my half-brother had approached them to tell of the abuse he had suffered at the hands of our stepmother over 30 years previously. I had little contact with him so had no idea that he had reached this stage of criminal proceedings. The police were gathering statements to determine whether there was enough evidence to prosecute my stepmother, Helen Ford. They told me that day to consider whether I wanted to be involved in the case – if I did, they would return to let me know what would happen next.

I felt as if I had been thrown into the eye of a storm.

Although it was incredible to me that someone was offering to listen to my story for the first time in my life, I was also terrified. I had locked so much of the abuse away for so long that I knew there would be enormous problems if I opened up those memories again. I was engaged and had my three wonderful children around me. None of these people knew what I had suffered. Did I want them to know the full horror of it?

After a great deal of soul searching, I decided to give my story to the authorities. I gave evidence at Helen Ford's trial and I quietly rejoiced when she was sentenced to imprisonment when found guilty of 'procuring a minor'.

In the days after the trial, I was approached by many journalists who wanted to write about my story. While many of them seemed supportive and friendly, something didn't quite feel right. Finally, I realised what it was. After years spent in silence, years spent being controlled by others, I was uncomfortable at the thought of someone else – another stranger – taking my words and being able to make the ultimate decision as to how those words would be presented.

After the trial, I was living with my dear friend, Christine, and her husband at their home in North Berwick. During the trial, I had thought about the possibility of writing a book – I had even mentioned I might do so to my half-brother and his wife over lunch one day. I didn't know how I was going to go about it, but I just knew I had to tell all of my story, every last bit of it, and not just what was likely to be published in a newspaper.

One day, I was speaking on the phone to a woman who ran a charity for survivors of sexual abuse. This woman and her organisation had been very helpful, and she was someone who sometimes 'filtered' journalists' requests to speak to survivors. That morning, she was passing on details of someone who wanted to do an interview about my story. I was cautious and said this to her, briefly bringing up the point that I really wanted to speak to someone who was in the industry and knew how the media and publishing worked – not for an interview, but to see whether my idea of doing a book was feasible. She said that she knew just the person, a journalist whom she had worked with a lot and seemed to understand the issues rather than just be looking for the next headline.

A meeting was set up at Christine's house, but I was still very nervous as it is hard for me to trust people. I also tend to go on my gut feelings, however, so as soon as I met the writer, Linda, I knew she was a good person. She was clear and concise when answering the questions I posed, and she didn't patronise me. In fact, she spent as much time warning me of some of the hurdles I might face as she did talking about what I might get from going down the publishing route. I felt that we hit it off really quickly and she didn't see me as some sort of victim.

The conversation we had about our children was the final push I needed to know that we would make a good team. The way she spoke about her family made me trust her because I knew she was a good mother. That's how I gauge women. If they are good mothers, they are trustworthy. I told her that I needed to explain everything that had happened to me in my own life, both for my own sake and for that of my kids. From that moment, I believed in her because she also believed in me, and she's never let me down. We both found a new friend that day.

I knew what I had to do.

I had to tell my story in full, by myself. It was time for me to write my book.

To do that, I've had to face all of my demons. I've had to look at things from my past that I'd hoped at one time to just bury away. It's been so hard, so painful and truly testing, yet as I write this, I am sitting in my home overlooking the Firth of Forth, with my three children, all happy, content and safe with their worlds. I feel truly blessed.

When I first told my story I was concerned with the immediate criminal element of it – the abuses committed against me by my stepmother and her friends when I was a little girl. But there is so much more to my story than her, than just Helen Ford.

うわ

I was born in a basement tenement in Edinburgh's Easter Road on 5 June 1959. At the time, my father, Donald Chalmers Ford, was living with my biological mother, Breda Curran Robertson. Breda had two children from two previous relationships, and was a young Irish lass who had come over the sea from Tipperary with her slightly older brother in the early 1950s. Sometime between arriving in Britain and meeting my father, she had given birth to her first child, a daughter, out of wedlock. She then went on to marry a different man and give birth a few years later to a son. Where and how she met my father is one of the many enigmas in my story, as is the question of whether or not they were truly in love before they consummated their relationship and conceived me. The foursome lived together in this flat in Easter Road, where I was born, until I was around a year old. At that point, my mother split from my father, and also left him with three children under six, two of whom were not his biological offspring. Why she left and where she went is a matter for speculation. I haven't seen her since that day and will probably never see her again.

So, when I was born, I already had this older half-brother and half-sister waiting for me. I have no memories of them in the very early days, although I have seen photographs of the three of us sitting together before we were admitted to Haldane House, the Barnardo's home we finally lived in. My half-brother, Simon, was two years older than me, and my half-sister, Frances, four years older. When my Dad met my mother, she was still married to Simon's father. In fact, she never married my Dad, nor was she married to the father of my half-sister.

It was October 1960 when my mother left. Disappeared. I have had to get a lot of my own story from various files collected from different sources over the years. From one of those files I know that:

> *On 6th October 1960, Ford* [my father] *reported to us* [the Scottish Society for the Prevention of Cruelty to Children] *that he had returned from England where he had been working to find Mrs Robertson* [my mother] *had been drinking, and having undesirable people in his home, and the*

*children and house neglected. They quarrelled, and Mrs
Robertson cleared out with another married woman and two
men, and although we have endeavoured to trace her our
efforts have been unsuccessful.*

The bald facts are that my mother upped and left and we were
alone with my father. I had known only one Dad, but my older
half-sister had known three men to take that role by this point,
and my half-brother two. It must have been very confusing for
the three of us already, and here we now were without a mummy
either.

My father continued to look after us with the help of a young
local girl while he went out to work. Sometimes this young girl
would take us to, and drop us off at, nursery. An entry in my files
from back then states:

*Miss Robertson (from Pilrig Nursery) has great admiration
for the father whom she has watched running home in
between shifts, doing without breakfast sometimes to take the
children to nursery, and who seems devoted to the children.
The girl who sometimes brings them did not appeal to Miss
Robertson who thought her unsuitable and rather unstable.
On one occasion the girl brought the children to the nursery
at 7.30am and left them in the charge of the cleaners until
opening at 8.30am.*

This extract chills me to the bone as the young girl in question is
Helen Gourlay, the woman who was to become my stepmother.
This arrangement of her helping out lasted for a while, then my
Dad decided he could no longer cope and we were taken into
care. For the next four years, the three of us stayed in a
Barnardo's home near Alloa in Scotland. At that time, it wasn't
only orphans or children whose parents would never want
anything to do with them who were put into homes. Barnardo's

also 'helped out' in situations where families needed a bit of time to get themselves together before reclaiming their children, before the final, desired act of 'restoration' as they called it.

I can only guess that my father couldn't do what he needed to do. When Breda left, he presumably thought that he would be able to work and also care for three young children. He probably did try but it wasn't enough, and there must have come a point where he had to admit defeat and send us away. Of course, I can question why he did this, why he didn't even decide to keep me, his only biological child, but – like everything else – I won't get any answers. How much the 'young girl' in the picture, Helen Gourlay, had a hand in our departure, I can't say.

But given what she was to reveal of herself in the years to come, I can guess . . .

Chapter Two

ॐ

MUMMIES AND DADDY

IN DECEMBER 1961 MY FATHER married this girl and in November 1962 they had a son, Gordon, who was another half-brother for me. There really is so much that I'm not aware of and will probably never find out. However, what I do know now is far more than I knew back in 2001, before I made the decision to go ahead and give that statement to the police which would be what they needed to finally press charges against Helen Gourlay Ford. Much of that knowledge came from just remembering and by looking over old documents, then putting all of the pieces together. My own life is a jigsaw to me, and I've had to approach putting it all together with very little 'inside' information.

My earliest memories are not of Breda, my biological mother – in fact, I have absolutely no memories of her at all, which is hardly surprising since she left my father when I was just a baby. No, my earliest memories are of my time in that Barnardo's children's home, of being one of many kids in the same position – parentless. I remember very clearly the amount of queuing which went on in that place, for everything from meals to baths to pocket money. I remember being hugged. I remember having fun. I remember laughing. I remember playing in big rambling gardens, but, most of all, I remember my Dad visiting me with piles of comics in his arms each time. I can still see the picture in my mind's eye of waiting in a great big sitting room for him to arrive, and feeling so excited that, today, I was one of the lucky ones who had a visitor – and not only that, not just any old visitor, this was my very own Dad!

Don Ford was quite a small man, around 5 foot 7 inches I would guess. He had, at that time, the blackest hair which was Brylcreemed and combed just so in a very particular way. He always wore a white shirt and a dark suit, and, like many men of his generation, his shoes were polished so that you could see your face in them. He told me when I was older that this was because he had been in the army. He said that a good soldier always paid particular attention to his shoes, and also said I should 'never forget to look behind', referring to making sure I polished the back of my shoes as well as the front.

There is very little else I remember about those visits from him to me in Barnardo's. I don't recall him hugging me or saying anything like 'I love you'. In fact, he never ever said those words to me at any point of his life. To tell the truth, he said very little about anything that actually mattered in all the years he was my Daddy. But, at that point, he was there on visit days and that was all that mattered.

My memories of my time in Barnardo's start to have more colour as time went on. A young girl began to accompany Dad on his trips. I know now that she was the one who had helped out and taken us to nursery. However, I didn't have any memories of those days so, to me, she was a stranger. I know now that my Dad was planning to make her his wife. I know now that she was my tormentor. Her presence on those visits is a bit blurry because she never paid any attention to me. She'd sit by my father's side, looking around, never smiling, never interacting with me at all, but, as time went on, I got used to her.

I was only about four years old when she appeared one day,

not only with my Dad, but with a baby in her arms too. It was a little boy, and Helen was a changed woman around him. She laughed and gurgled at him; she blew raspberries and sang him songs. She looked happy. I had been told that this little boy was my baby brother, and I was small enough myself to just accept that. He may have been a link between me and my father, but it was purely biological – that tiny boy would turn out to be my tormentor, just like his mother.

Apart from noticing Helen and the baby, the next most vivid memory I have of Don Ford is when he came to collect me from Barnardo's and take me home to live with him, his new wife and their son. It was July 1964. I was five years and one month old and I was so excited because I was going home with my Daddy! That time with him is one of the nicest memories I would ever have of us being together. As I waited at the window of the children's home, looking out with my little suitcase at my feet, there was a moment full of hope and unspoken love. My Daddy was coming for me; he was taking me home. We would be a family and everything would be perfect, just like it was in story books.

I would never feel that pure optimism and brightness again at any point of my childhood. Nothing bad had happened to me at that stage. I lived in a children's home, but I knew no different. I looked forward to my Daddy's visits, but now I was bursting with delight at the thought of having him in my world full time. The people in Barnardo's had looked after me well – as well as they could manage given the circumstances – and I had no reason to expect that my world would be anything other than what I hoped for.

I'd learn.

I held my Daddy's hand as we journeyed all the way from Alloa on two trains and a bus to our home in Edinburgh. It would never get better than that trip. I would have stayed on those trains, that bus, for ever, clasping his fingers in mine all the while if I had known even a fraction of what lay in wait for me.

The Daddy who chatted with me and told me all about the sights on our way home, who told me that I was going home to a new Mummy and baby brother and that everything would be lovely, rarely emerged again in all the years we were together. Since I left home as a teenager, and since I have reflected on my life, I have asked myself the same questions over and over again: where did that man go, and why did he change? As my abuse became worse and worse, why did he let things go on? Did he really see nothing? Did he just ignore it all for an easy life, or was he too under the control of Helen? He never gave me any answers. As I journeyed to womanhood, I was left to piece together a picture of that man, my father, and his role in my childhood. Who was my Daddy?

Chapter Three

꒛

ONE BIG, HAPPY FAMILY

MY EARLIEST MEMORIES OF BOTH Simon and Frances are from when we were in the children's home together. As we were different ages, we slept in separate dorms but we would meet up in the play room, dining room or sitting room. Even then, there were lots of other children around. My recollections of how we interacted then are not strong. I have only fleeting glimpses in my mind of us being together, and that was on the occasions when my Dad and Helen visited us with baby Gordon. It was 1964 when I returned home to live with my Dad and his new wife. A year later, Simon and Frances returned. These are the memories that are the strongest for me.

I knew that they were returning because there had been a lot of talk about it during the run-up to them coming 'home'. I was really looking forward to it because I was already feeling quite isolated in the house. Helen only had time for her little boy and there was never a nice word from her. On the contrary, she had already started beating me and sending me to my room for long periods of time. I thought when my big sister and brother came home she would stop. I also believed that I would finally have someone to play with as I wasn't allowed to play with Gordon in case I hurt Helen's precious boy. I certainly wasn't allowed to play with his toys.

On 5 March 1965, Frances and Simon were brought home by my Dad. During the first week or so of their return, our Auntie Madge, Uncle Alec, Uncle George, Granny Ford (all from my Dad's family) visited, as did some of Helen's family, and it seemed as if things could be happy. Indeed, things were a little better for a while. I thought that my prayers had been answered and that Helen was really going to change. However, I soon found out that it wasn't for our sakes that she was being nice. I know now that it was all about her. Helen proudly showed us off and received bucketloads of praise for taking us all on.

I clearly remember walking along Easter Road one day. Helen was pushing the pram with her little boy sitting in it, while Simon and I held on to the chrome handle on either side of her. Frances was walking along beside me, holding my other hand. As we went from shop to shop, people would stop and talk to Helen and admire us all, telling Helen that she was doing brilliantly and that she was a saint for taking us all on. Little did anyone know what she was really like behind closed doors.

꒕

I don't remember exactly when things started changing but before long it seemed as if there was a turnaround in Helen's attitude to all of us. I expected it, as I knew what she had been like before they came home, but they were not at all prepared for her cruelty. I have no memories of fun and play; I just remember the beatings and punishments.

What I find most shocking is that this young woman, who was barely 21 years old and hardly mature herself, had been given responsibility for three vulnerable children. My own daughter is this age now. When I look at Claire, who is a wonderful person, and think about any 21-year-old being given such control in the way that Helen was, I shudder. I know this would be highly unlikely to happen now, but it did to us, and I do have to point the finger at the people who ultimately had control over our fates. We were in the care of the local authority because our needs were not being met, yet we were sent to live with a young woman who had not been properly vetted; to a house that had one small bedroom and a living room with a scullery. We were so vulnerable and this woman played on our vulnerability. I cannot understand her motives for wanting to take us all on, and I cannot help being cynical about what they might have been, given what we were to endure.

Reading through my files, I found that there were many issues about money from the time my mother left. Apparently, she'd left many debts. I also know that while we were in Barnardo's, a contribution towards our keep had to be paid by my Dad to the authority concerned. One document states:

> *We shall require Mr Ford to contribute at the rate of 8/- per week each for the older boy and girl and 10/- per week for Donna . . . covered by the family allowance.*

Of course, when we went to live with them not only did my Dad and Helen then receive the family allowance for us, but they were also paid for the 'fostering' of Simon.

Whatever her reasons for taking us on, financial or otherwise, it was clear that Helen was very resentful of the responsibility we brought, and that she didn't like us. My sister and I were often attacked by her for our looks. I know now that I was a pretty little girl (although it has been a long, hard journey to realising that) and so was my sister, but Helen did everything in her power to make sure that we thought we were horrible. We were told that we were ugly over and over again, and one of Helen's favourite methods of physical abuse was to grab me by the hair and ram my face up against the mirror. In time to each thrust into the glass, she would shout: 'Look at you! You are so ugly! Ugly!

Ugly! Ugly!' It's hard not to believe this sort of thing when it is drummed into you time and time again.

In particular, I was so happy to have my big sister home to stay. Frances was beautiful. She had the longest dark hair and the prettiest face – in fact, she reminded me of Snow White. It wasn't long after she returned from Haldane House that Helen sat her down in the living room on one of the wooden dining chairs. She calmly placed a bowl on Frances's head and cut off all of her beautiful hair. She butchered my big sister. I remember crying as I swept the hair up and held it, touching its softness and darkness as I put it in the bin. Helen's face was a picture of smugness and contentment as she looked at Frances – she had managed to transfer some of her own ugliness onto my beautiful sister.

I loved Frances so much. She would hug me and play with me, and when I cried would wipe the tears from my eyes. Simon was different – he looked confused most of the time and was both shy and nervous.

We had a social worker who visited us every four to six weeks. Prior to these visits, Helen would sit us down on the settee in a row. She would point at a little brass ornament of three monkeys which sat on the mantelshelf and she would say to us, 'That's the three of you. See no evil, speak no evil and hear no evil. If the social worker asks you if you're happy, you tell her yes! If she asks if I am good to you, say yes!' She would stand behind the social worker as she spoke to us and glower at us with what we called the 'evil eye'. We really stood no chance. We were powerless to question this woman's actions towards us. Although Helen's strictness was observed, it wasn't investigated further. In one report from those days, the social worker writes:

> *Mrs Ford is quite strict with the children . . . There is a tendency for the three older children to stand to attention.*

It was noticed then that we were treated differently from Gordon, but it wasn't followed through.

~

Any normal bonding that should have occurred between me and my half-siblings was thwarted at every turn by Helen. We had different schools, different doctors and different dentists. With regard to punishments, she gave us pretty much similar beatings but always kept us separate when doing so, presumably to stop us knowing too much or ganging up on her.

I have one strong memory of Simon and I getting into trouble for something. I can't remember what it was, but I do recall the two of us standing in the living room in front of the fire with our hands by our sides while Helen shouted at us. My brother was then told to go into the bathroom and I was to wait outside. Helen came through minutes later with the belt and went into the bathroom. I could hear Simon being beaten. I heard every whack of the belt as she shouted at him. He was to say sorry, she kept screaming, and to say that he was bad. I was terrified because I knew it was almost my turn – and indeed it was. After Helen had beaten us, both in our underwear, we were each made to stand in separate places; he in the recess in the lobby and me in the bathroom.

While this went on, my sister was in the living room looking after the baby. It wasn't that she was a favourite in any way – she got her share of beatings too – but a lot of the time Helen used her for babysitting or other chores and keeping things together while she whacked us other two. Even in the files there is a mention of Frances coming back from the launderette with the family wash when she was just 10 years old.

This was the pattern of the contact between Frances, Simon and I for the duration that Helen was living with my father. My sister got out sooner than us, however. There's a great deal of speculation about how and why she left, and I know only a few things. I do know that when she went she was around 15 years of age and she was taken back into care. I know for a fact that my father would not speak to Frances after she left because there had been some 'accusations'. What those accusations were I do not know, but she left. I saw her only once after that when I was around 16 and she would have been 20. She was living in a flat in the Meadows.

I feel so sad for the little girl my sister was and for the little boy my brother was. I wish I had some memories to call on of being with them both, of playing with them and laughing with them, but sadly I have only memories of a desperate sense of isolation from each of us. It was sink or swim under the 'care' of Helen, and we each had to look out for ourselves, although I was the one she seemed particularly keen to break.

Chapter Four

‒ᗡ‒

WHAT MIGHT HAVE BEEN

HELEN FORD WAS UNDOUBTEDLY TO blame for the vast majority of the absolute horrors that were inflicted on me as a little girl, but there have to be questions asked about my father as well. Who had Donald Ford been, and was there anything in his past that could have made him the pathetic excuse for a father he would turn out to be?

Before meeting my mother, Breda, my Dad had spent some time in the forces after being conscripted. I recall seeing some small black-and-white photographs of him during his time in the army, in which he looked very smart and happy. He had also trained as a French polisher, and still did odd jobs in that line when he was asked. In fact, the table that had once belonged to his mother, and which I would see once he took me home, had been polished by him and he would proudly show people his handiwork.

I still own a jewellery box that he made. It is one of only two things he ever gave me (the other thing is a set of brass letter scales my Auntie Nellie gave him). I'm not sure whether the box is teak or mahogany, but it's about six inches long and four inches high. It has a wood veneer on the top with a paler inlay of a simple line pattern. I was given the box while I was still at home. My Dad told me that it was his apprentice piece, and that he had made it from scratch. I have had it ever since and I use it now to keep foreign coins in from my travels to Greece, Portugal, France, South Africa, Jamaica, Turkey and India. I have kept this box because I have so very, very little from my childhood. Every tiny thing I did manage to keep – a couple of dinner tickets I wanted to hold on to and a few other bits – have all been put into this innocuous little box. I have never questioned why until writing this now, but I suppose in a way I have kept it because it is something my Dad created before life came in and changed the young man he once was, the one I never got to know. I know what he did and what he didn't do for me, and I have no respect whatsoever for that man. However, I do like to think that at some point he was good, and so were his intentions. The box has always been with me, and if one of my girls wanted it they could certainly have it, but I don't think it would mean much to them.

So, my Dad did have a profession, which that jewellery box symbolises for me, yet when I came to stay with him and Helen in the Easter Road house, he was working on the corporation buses. I remember his work uniform and ticket machine, and I also remember getting to go with him on the number one bus when he was doing a shift one day. This was in the days when there were old buses with an open back, spiral stairs and wooden decking on the floor. Gallus – lively – young people would hold on to the metal pole, swing around it and then jump off before the bus stopped.

The next job he had was working for the General Post Office as a postman. They wore grey suits in those days with brass buttons stamped with GPO, and carried heavy sack bags. Sometimes he cycled to work on an old black bike. I remember going with him while he delivered letters, propped on the front of his bike while he cycled with two bags full of post slung over the back of it. Those were great times – me and my Dad together, as it should have been, as I'd dreamed it would be, but as it was, so rarely. But always, always, at the end of it, there was my return home to a living hell.

From these sparse recollections, I've gathered that he was conscientious and worked to look after his family. In the early days of my return from Barnardo's, he would always come home from work on a Friday with a brand new Matchbox car in its little box for my new brother. I was a bit jealous, but what I really wanted wasn't a gift. I didn't want anything material at all, and I still don't. All I ever wanted was love and a little bit of time spent together with the only parent I had, away from the madness of my days with Helen. I got it sometimes, but it was rare and precious.

I would sometimes go on walks with my Daddy to feed the ducks and throw a penny in the wishing well in Holyrood's Kings Park. Those days were lovely and he would always stop off at Casey's sweet shop at the top of Easter Road to buy a bag of mixed boilings. Casey's was a lovely old-fashioned family-run place. The smell of that little shop with its multicoloured rows of jars full of toffee doddles, bonbons, sweet-peanuts and kola cubes is one of the memories I hold dear to my heart. A visit there would always round off the day perfectly.

It hurts.

I want to know where that Daddy went, the Daddy who would hand me a sweetie from a white paper bag while telling me stories of old Edinburgh as we walked. He could do that – he had the capacity to be warm and loving, but it ended up becoming even rarer as time went on. I remember a party in the house shortly after I returned from the home. He was singing and laughing. All of his family were there: his two brothers and his sister, my granny and various other faces that I can't place so long after the event, and they had all come to meet me. I felt so proud, so loved and, in this memory, my Dad seems truly happy.

When I look back on this time – the sweet shops, the trips to the wishing well, the times alone with him – I think I can see my

Dad as he could have been, as he would have been, as he wasn't allowed to be. I know that his relationship with Helen was fraught, and I understand that what goes on between two people can never really be understood by outsiders. But I know some other things too. What went on and what happened to me as a result of him choosing to live with and marry that woman stole my childhood from me and, to this day, has repercussions on my identity and being.

He didn't protect me. He didn't take me to safety, away from her. He ignored and minimised what was happening. He closed his eyes tightly against the evil that would be wreaked on me for years and years. Evil that wouldn't leave just because Helen did.

Evil which has left me with a question that I still want to scream at him: Do you know what you did, Daddy? *Do you know what you did?*

༈

Chapter Five

HOME

IF I AM TO TRY AND understand my father's role in all of this, I have to go back to the beginning. And the beginning is painful for me. I had hope. I thought I was going to a family – my family – who would love me and protect me.

My initial reaction at seeing my new home is etched on my memory, even though I was so young. I'd been living in that large rambling children's home since I was a baby, but here I was being taken 'home' to a one-bedroom basement flat in a tenement block. Everything was so small. There was the one tiny bedroom, a bathroom and a living room with a bed recess at one end and a scullery at the other. The flat would have been big enough for a young married couple alone, but it was nowhere near spacious enough for a family of four – and it certainly wasn't the size required for the family of seven it would house within the next couple of years.

The living room itself doubled as a bedroom for my Dad and Helen. It had a double bed in the recess, where they slept, and in front of the post-war tiled fireplace sat a three-piece suite in dark-red embossed leatherette fabric. On the dark wooden sideboard against one wall was a black-and-white television, the same television I watched as Winston Churchill's funeral was broadcast.

There were two drawers in this sideboard that were full of cutlery. In the two cupboards below, cereal and biscuits and other foods jostled for space. I recall the smell of this cupboard more than any other because it was where the food was; food I was to be deprived of so often, for so long. In the window space, there was a table with chairs, which looked out on to the communal back garden, or back green as we called it.

Everything was cramped and claustrophobic compared to the vast rooms at the Barnardo's home. There was nearly always a coal fire lit as that was what heated the water by means of a back boiler. It soon became my job to clear the fireplace of ashes, and to roll and twist newspapers ready for the next lighting. Sitting in the hearth was a brass fireside companion set, complete with tongs and pokers. That would become another instrument of torture once Helen got going.

The one bedroom was used as the kids' room. When I arrived it already had a set of wooden bunk beds and a cot. There was a large window opposite the door and a fireplace to the side of it, over which hung a picture of Jesus whose eyes would follow every move of anyone in that room – or so it seemed to me. Under the window was a small chest of drawers and that was about it. This room, like all the other rooms in the house, was very neat but cramped. I suppose that I might have seen the place as cosy, had I been in the heart of a loving family. What 'could have been' may be a silly game to play, but sometimes it's hard to prevent yourself falling into that trap.

The rooms I have already described had their horrors, but the bathroom in this first house was to become my most dreaded room. It wasn't even appealing to begin with – it had a high ceiling and an old-fashioned deep cast-iron bath with a Victorian toilet and cistern complete with pull chain. I was soon to get to know every crack on every wall in this room, every embossed swirl on the frosted glass door, as I was made to stand in there for hours on end, starving, shaking and freezing with cold.

꒝

Food was to become a big issue for me as a child. I was soon regularly deprived of it by Helen, as one of her means of exerting control over me. It will come as no surprise, then, that I have really strong memories of the times I was actually fed. In those early days I remember the food Helen gave me. Breakfast would be a bowl of cornflakes with a cup of tea and some toast. Lunch would be something like soup with a pudding, perhaps rice or jam. Tea, as we called it, could be anything from mince and tatties to cold meat and chips, to my dreaded and most hated meal of all – tripe and onions.

Helen didn't just stop giving me food all of a sudden. It happened gradually. She would make me miss out on a meal for being naughty (in her eyes), which eventually led to me not knowing when I would next be fed. In fact, this was a pattern with my stepmother, as the abuse she was leading up to began in the same fashion. To start with, I would be told off for things I did – such as playing with toys that belonged to her son, speaking when not spoken to, taking a biscuit before being offered – and many other things she would just decide were bad from one day to the next.

There was, however, one type of behaviour so abhorrent to Helen that she placed it above all of my other so-called trans-gressions – and that was wetting the bed. Memories come flooding back to me sometimes when I least expect them to, and often they are things I've buried. One striking recollection I have is the terrible telling-off I would get for not going to the toilet in the middle of the night.

I did have a problem with this while I was in the children's home, and I remember the way it was dealt with there. On a Saturday all of the children would be gathered in the main room. They would sit down in little seats which had been placed in rows before a large table. Behind this table sat two or three members of staff who would hand out pocket money and sweets (usually homemade tablet) to each child. We would traipse up, say 'thank you' and return to our seats clutching our little stash. However, the children who had been naughty, for one reason or another, would be singled out, their crimes would be revealed and they would forfeit either their pocket money or their sweets – or both, depending on the severity of the crime. Wetting the bed was one of these crimes, as I knew full well. I remember the sheer embarrassment of sitting there and having my name called out, and then going without the trip to the shops to spend my money or without the only sweet treat of the week.

As the years went by and I worked in children's homes as an adult, I encountered many youngsters who wet their beds, and I gained more insight into the problem. There are so many reasons why a child may suffer from this very common complaint, including lack of control over bladder function, sleep apnoea and stress. What I experienced in the children's home in the 1960s was due to ignorance rather than cruelty – but this can't be said of Helen's attitude and punishment.

When I first went to stay with her and my Daddy, she would just change the sheets and my pyjamas if I had an 'accident', then get me up to go to the toilet during the night. But I kept wetting the bed and this made Helen angrier and angrier. Any little bit of patience she had in her soon wore off. Eventually, I was the one who had to get up and take the sheets off my bed and trample them in the bath along with my pyjamas. I also had to wash down with disinfectant the red rubber mat that covered my mattress. When my stepmother was finally at the end of her tether – it was a short one – she made me lie on this rubber mat with no sheet, clad only in my pants, and sleep that way night after night. She would come in to check on me – it seemed as if she was willing it to happen – and then hiss in my face: 'Pee-the-bed, pee-the-bed – nasty little pee-the-bed, aren't you?' She liked nicknames and her preferred one for me then was 'pissy pants'.

By the time my older half-siblings arrived back from the children's home, I was just past my sixth birthday and still wetting the bed. Looking back, it's hardly surprising. I had been treated the Barnardo's way when the problem started, and that approach clearly hadn't been designed to resolve the issue, but now there wasn't even any pretence that I was going to be helped. It had been bad enough to face ridicule at home from Helen, but once I started school, she made me wear my wet, smelly knickers there all day. Children are often cruel to each other, and they will pick on anything different, so I became the focus of their taunts as they said I smelled, they said I smelled of piss, they said I was wearing dirty pants.

They were right.

When Helen was really angry with me, she would come into the bedroom first thing in the morning and drag me out of bed by my arms. 'Stand there!' she'd screech at me as I stood where she had put me. 'Stand there and don't you dare move!' She'd throw the thin covers right back so that she could inspect the bottom sheet and mattress. If I had wet them, she would shout and scream at the top of her voice, while hitting me repeatedly with her fists and arms. When this frenzy had passed to some extent, Helen would pull my pants off and rub my face in them, grinding me into the stinking material with utter hatred. Finally, as she prepared to leave the room, she would throw the knickers at me and say that I was to put them on. I'd have to go to school wearing them, with my face stinging and red, and the smell of pee hanging around me for the rest of the day. No-one else at home got treated like that – maybe no-one else wet the bed. I only saw her do anything similar to our dog, Snooky, a black-and-white mongrel collie cross. If Snooky ever had an accident in the house, his face would be rubbed in it and he would be kicked out into the back green with a yelp. My stepmother clearly thought I was as low as the dog.

When I became a mother, these memories sometimes crept through. I could never imagine why anyone would do the things

Helen had done to me. Even the fact that I wasn't related to her by blood didn't explain why she felt such hatred for me. How any adult could do those things to a child was beyond me. If my daughters or son ever wet the bed, I would run them a bath and, while they were in the big, soapy bubbles, I would get their sheets and pyjamas into the wash without a word to them. I'd remind myself to watch what they drank before bedtime and to lift them for the toilet before I went to bed.

This was certainly not Helen's way. I was a child, little more than a baby, when I was delivered into the care of Helen and my father. Of course, I didn't keep a diary, and I don't have a photographic memory, and so my awareness of when things happened can't be precise. However, I do know that there was a switch, very early on in my life at Easter Road, when Helen changed from being cold and distant to being hateful and violent. This was around the time when she started to berate me constantly for being 'really bad'. And that 'badness' was something Helen always thought could be beaten out of me.

꒜

One day, when I was about six, I had been really bad – as usual. I know that it was before my half-brother and half-sister came back from Barnardo's. I don't know why it had been decided that I was bad that day (I rarely did), but I had been told to spend the whole morning and afternoon in the bathroom, in my underwear, with my hands by my sides. I wasn't allowed to move an inch.

Not an inch.

As I write this, I can almost feel what it was like that day when I was hurt so much – not physically, but emotionally. It hurt more than anything Helen ever did to me because I loved my Daddy at this point. I looked up to him, he was my hero – and he was going to fail me.

'Wait till your father gets home,' Helen hissed in my ear.

'Wait till your father gets home,' she shouted into my face.

It was her mantra for hours and I did as I was told. I did wait. I did wait until my father got home. But even though I had no idea whatsoever of what I had done that was so 'bad', there was still a little part of me that thought, 'Well, when my Daddy does get home, he'll know that I'm a good girl, and he'll know that Helen is lying. He'll know this because he's my Daddy.'

I waited and waited.

I was almost numb with cold and stiff from the lack of moving around when I finally heard him coming in the front door. I listened to his footsteps walking up the lobby into the living room. I felt relief. My Daddy was home, and I hadn't had all hope kicked out of me yet. I thought that he would tell me to come through, have some tea, get my pyjamas on and go to bed. At first, I heard the muffled voices of him and Helen talking, then I heard him coming to the bathroom door.

When he came in, I almost shouted out, 'Daddy!' but he grabbed me by the wrist so quickly that I didn't have a chance. 'Why are you being so bad?' he asked me. 'Why are you being so bad, Donna?' He kept on asking me that question as he pulled me by the wrist through to the bedroom. 'Your Mummy is trying her best with you, but you have to be good,' he said. I tried to tell him that I was, I was good, but I was crying so much that I couldn't get the words out. My Daddy sat on the lower bunk bed, pulled me over his knee and then he hit me and hit me over and over again on the bottom. I kept saying, through the sobs, 'I will be good, Daddy, I am trying to be good,' but it was as if he couldn't hear me. Finally, he stopped and said that it had hurt him more than it had hurt me. He told me that I had to be good for my Mummy and that I was to stop giving her trouble, then told me to go to bed. He finished by saying that he didn't want to come home the next day and find out that I had been 'bad' again.

That became a pattern; it set the trend for many more occasions. Helen had now convinced my Dad that I was bad, and by the number of occasions he beat me, I could only assume he believed her. On many more occasions throughout my childhood I was to discover my father's wrath, always induced by Helen. I know that she was behind it because when she left he stopped beating me. If only she could have taken the memories away with her too.

Chapter Six

જી

CHASTISEMENT

THERE ARE SPECIFIC TIMES I remember when my Dad would repeat this pattern – he would come home from work, talk to Helen then come to 'chastise' me.

That was the word he used.

During the very early days of my return home, I would sometimes find the courage to speak up and question why I was being smacked. Why did Helen say I was bad? Why did I get shouted at? Why did I have to go to bed? Why did I have to stand naked in the bathroom for hours? To begin with, I could ask these questions because sometimes my Dad would just give me a talking to on his return home from work. I was trying to make sense of Helen's rules and expectations of me. I was trying to work out what I'd done during the day that made Helen shout and yell to my Dad about how bad I'd been. I didn't realise that there was no real rhyme or reason to it. She was just evil.

When he came home, I'd usually be in my bedroom, having been sent there at some point during the day. On some days I might have been in my bedroom for hours, alone and starving. On other occasions I was sent to my room just minutes before my Dad came in so he wouldn't see me standing in the bath, naked, freezing, facing the wall. Generally, I'd be sitting on my bed, having been crying my eyes out, and my Daddy would come in and stand over me. Over and over again he'd ask me: 'Why? Why? Why?'

How could I answer him?

I rarely knew what had brought about Helen's punishment in the first place, so how could I work out why I would deliberately choose to be bad? I didn't want to disappoint my Daddy though, so I always said that I'd be good, even if I didn't really know what I was agreeing to. I wanted to be. Whatever being good would involve, I wanted to be that way. I wanted to be good like my new brother; I wanted to be hugged and played with; I wanted to be brought home a toy car on a Friday night by my Daddy, just like little Gordon was. When I asked him through my tears why I was always getting rows and punishments, why I was always being sent to bed, he said he had to 'chastise' me because it would help me to be good. But the 'chastisement' increased. The smacking got harder and harder as my Dad got angrier and angrier – and, in time, he moved on to using his belt against me as well. I couldn't defend myself. I was tiny and any protests were ignored. Finally, I wasn't even allowed to voice any murmurs of dissent at all.

I don't ever remember him 'chastising' the children he had with Helen, although I do know that she encouraged him to hit my elder half-siblings too. Of course, I now realise that this violence was a direct reaction to what Helen told him every time: I had been bad all day; I had been horrible to her; I was a vile child; I hated my younger brother; I was the catalyst. It was all me, and his version of chastisement increasingly became a way of him venting his anger and frustration.

Looking back, I can only imagine how it must have been for this man. He must have hurt after my mother left him, and he must have been doing everything in his power to maintain his relationship with Helen. I was there putting a spoke in the big wheel with my badness, and he believed her – why wouldn't he?

He didn't know me. On top of that, practically every day he had Helen in his face straight after work, telling him the stories she had made up about me. How ironic that it was actually Helen who had been up to all sorts, things he had absolutely no idea of – if she'd been having one of her parties, she'd be trying to hide the fact, or coping with being a bit drunk.

My Dad always worked long hours, leaving really early in the morning before we were even up, and not returning home until after 4pm. When he worked overtime, which was more often than not, he sometimes wouldn't return until about 10 o'clock at night. He hardly seemed to be home.

The times we saw most of him were during the summer holidays. He would usually take off the 'trades' fortnight', the first two weeks in July when, in those days, most of the factories and businesses in the city would close for two weeks. Everyone knew that during these two weeks you couldn't get a workman for love nor money, and it was the time when most families would leave for their annual trip to the seaside. In our case, we would go to Kinghorn in Fife, where we would stay in a wooden chalet and spend the days exploring the beaches and caves. These times were, on the whole, good but, as always, Helen had to retain control. Even on holiday she took a belt with her to use on me. I was forced to stand for hours in the bedroom with its two sets of bunk beds. The curtains would be closed and I could hear the sound of children whooping and laughing outside.

I have to ask myself what my Dad was doing on those days. He wasn't at work and he didn't have the excuse of not seeing how Helen operated. From what I can remember, he spent most of his holiday in the clubhouse. I can imagine it must have involved beer, dominoes, horse racing and being away from Helen and her moods. I have one good image of my Dad taking me fishing on one holiday. We caught sticklebacks that were too big for the little metal pail I had. They were catching their tails as they swam, turning round and round in circles, never getting anywhere. My Dad watched them for ages, mesmerised – maybe he saw his own existence within their futile endeavours. Thinking of him that way is nice as it was so normal, but I have far more memories of him coming back from the club smelling of beer, and arguing with Helen as soon as he returned, the sound echoing around the wooden walls. Even there, in that lovely place, there were always arguments. In fact, arguments seemed to be about all they had in common.

Occasionally, when Frances was still at home, my Dad and Helen would go off to the club together in the evening, leaving us all in bed with strict instructions not to move. Time out together was pretty rare for them – perhaps because Helen much preferred to party without the presence of her husband, as I would find out to my cost.

So, you see, I was never bad. I was just a child with basic needs that weren't being met. I was hungry. I was cold. I was battered. I was unloved. I tried to state my case but whenever I plucked up the courage to speak, I was accused of being cheeky, insolent, rude. I couldn't make sense of any of it, but even without that understanding, I soon learned how to deal with my daily abuse.

I learned not to talk.

I learned not to scream or cry when I was beaten.

I learned not to question any adult's actions towards me.

And now I can see that was exactly what Helen wanted.

I soon learned that, when any form of abuse came at me, I should just take it, with the knowledge that it would soon be over.

Wouldn't it?

As an adult, I can see now that Helen was grooming me. She was a good teacher – she taught me how to behave; she taught me that if I yelled or wept or questioned her, the punishment would be more severe. There was one occasion when she was beating me over and over again with the belt in the bathroom and

I jumped away and fell. While I was crouching down by the toilet, she hit me with even more fury, belting and belting me over the head, back, shoulders – wherever she could – screaming at me the whole time for being disobedient. I couldn't get up. I had my arms crossed over my face as I was screaming: 'Don't, Mummy! Please don't, Mummy! I'll be good, I'll be good!' As she hit me, she screamed, 'I'm not your Mummy! I'm not your fucking Mummy and I never will be! Don't you dare call me that!' She kept going until she'd spent herself. She walked away and I was just left there, in a heap on the floor, shaking, until I was told to go to bed.

~

Chapter Seven

SUCH A GOOD MAN

I SPENT MANY YEARS BLOCKING out my past and these terrible times. When I was first asked to give a statement to the police about my stepmother, I was reluctant to go back there – because I was scared. Initially, I could only remember some fragmented things. However, once I started remembering – once I started digging – it was like opening the floodgates. One memory would trigger off another; even here, as I relate one story, another will soon come to me. When I first started remembering it was too painful to look at. It was horrible; it was like going back in there; the pain was excruciating. Now, although the memories still hurt, they are not quite as profound as they once were. I put that down to being able to tell my story, being able to get it all out.

Just as I've thought of the story of my time in the bathroom, being beaten by Helen, I've remembered another instance of being thrashed in there. The bathroom door was open and I could see Snooky, the dog, sitting in the hall. I never really got on with that dog because he was always treated better than I was. Whereas I got little or no food, he was always fed a full tin of dog meat every day plus biscuits; he even had his own chocolate drops which were kept in the cupboard under the sink beside the pots and pans. I ate some of these from time to time when I was doing the dishes and had to put the saucepans away. Snooky was allowed to lie on the rug in front of the fire, and he was petted and loved. He even got to go out. I envied that dog and the life he led.

Anyway, on this particular day I was bent over the bath in my underwear. Helen started beating me, telling me to say that I was sorry, that I was bad, that I deserved to be punished. I was trying my hardest to remain in the same position as Helen had demanded, but it was so sore that I eventually squirmed around as she hit me. At one particular whack, I let out a scream. Snooky leapt up and ran into the bathroom where he started barking and snapping at me. Helen continued to whack at my little body as the dog sank his teeth into my stomach. I couldn't make sense of it – I was about seven years old, how could I?

꙳

I don't want to make excuses for my father but neither do I want to criticise him unnecessarily. All I want to do here is understand him a bit more. He is no longer alive so I can't speak to him face to face about this multifaceted story which is so far from straightforward, but I do need to work through what I know. I have very few good memories of him, and these are mixed up with some memories where I feel sorry for him. I know how ineffective he was at seeing what Helen was putting me through, but, in my mind's eye, I also see how kind he could be at times.

He was forever helping people out. After Helen left we always had people staying over, people who had been chucked out of their homes, always men. I know that he just wanted to help these men, but most of them abused this kindness by abusing me. I recall people saying that he was such a good man for looking after all of us in the way he did. Most men, they said, would run a mile. This seeped into my subconscious and affected how I thought of him. For many years, I just couldn't see that my father was as responsible for my childhood treatment as Helen was. I suppose he was the better of the two in many ways, and he certainly never sexually abused me directly. However, by making the conscious decision to take me from Barnardo's to live with my stepmother and him, he was responsible to a large extent.

He was my father.

I was his little girl.

He should have protected me.

※

While Helen was still with my Dad, I didn't see much of him apart from the times he was asked to 'deal with' me. One particular incident that sticks in my mind happened shortly after we moved to Edina Place in 1967, when I would be seven or eight years old. It must have been a school holiday because I was at home but my Dad wasn't. This day was like most. I heard Helen get up and move about, make tea, switch the radio on, blaring out the latest hits. I heard her feed her children. Meanwhile, I lay frozen in bed waiting for her first command. It came this particular morning with a thump, thump, thump as she banged on my bedroom door. 'You! Get up! Get out of bed, NOW!' she screamed. I did as I was told (I always did), and then I stood behind the door, trembling, waiting for her next order.

There were chores every single day: the dishes, sweeping up, washing the woodwork, scrubbing the floors, polishing the linoleum, cleaning out the fire, polishing the brass, bringing in the coal, taking out the rubbish – anything that needed to be done I and my older half-siblings would have to do. My most hated job was cleaning out the toilet. I had to pour bleach down it, then, with a cloth, I'd put my hand into the water and scrub every inch of the thing until it was 'spotless'.

Then there was trampling the blankets. I didn't really mind this chore if I was left alone to do it, but Helen was in a bad mood that day. I was dragged from my bedroom by the hair and smacked across the face with the back of her hand for looking at her 'like that'. I never knew what 'that' was. I know now she just hated me and having to be a parent to me – those things and the fact that I was my father's firstborn were my real crimes. There was never any rhyme or reason to Helen's behaviour or mood swings. She could go from being quite chirpy and offering me food or the chance to get out and do the shopping or to brush her hair (which I hated), to this.

That day, I was dragged into the bathroom and ordered to fill the bath, with Helen reminding me that cold water would be good enough. Then I put the bleach and blankets in. The bleach gave off such a stench it made my eyes sting, and I knew my skin would be red and irritated afterwards – but those things were the least of my worries. The smell of bleach is often a trigger for me, bringing back a memory of those times. I hate swimming pools for this reason.

Trampling the sheets or blankets was usually a once-a-week event as Helen was very particular about keeping a clean house. The bedroom she shared with my Dad – which was wholly out of bounds to me – was immaculate, and the amount of cleaning we each had to do daily ensured the rest of the house matched. I don't think she was obsessed by it; I just think she liked the praise she got for the effort. I remember the look of pride on her face when one social worker commented on what a nice tidy house she kept. The woman jokingly questioned how Helen managed it with all those children. Little did she know that it was us who kept it that way; maybe she could have dug just a little deeper rather than make light of it.

So that day, first thing in the morning and before breakfast (which I was never guaranteed to get anyway), Helen was standing there beside me in the bathroom in a nylon quilted dressing gown combined with the worn leather slippers she always had on her feet. Her eyes were magnified by her NHS glasses and her false teeth clicked furiously in her mouth as she screamed at me: 'Get in the fucking bath, you useless little bastard!' I did everything that she said without hesitating, as I always did. I trampled the blankets in the bath, walking up and down until she was satisfied that I was doing my job properly and could continue unsupervised. She left me to get on with it. I heard her boys going out to play for the day, bouncing their football down the lobby as they went, and I heard Helen move about in the living room. I carried on with my task, trampling up and down the bath, squeezing all the muck out of the blankets as my spindly legs got bluer and bluer with the cold water. As I trampled, I imagined that I was in Kinghorn, on holiday again, and that I was really splashing through the waves looking out for the baby flounders that lay just under the sand.

I was rudely awakened from that thought when Helen yelled at me to 'get wringing'. This meant I now had to drain the water out of the bath, rinse the blankets then wring the water out by twisting the wet blankets. I was never a big child – Helen made sure of that by starving me – and that task is a difficult enough one for an adult. For me, with my tiny frame, it was nearly impossible. I was supposed to get all the water out, enough for them to be taken down to the back green to be hung out to dry. I did my best and folded them as well as I could before putting them in the plastic wash basket in the bath ready for Helen. I went back to my room as instructed and waited there for my next order. I was obviously not getting breakfast that day. My only hope of food some mornings was if I was on dishwashing duty and could scavenge a leftover from the plates of the others.

I could hear Helen going about her business while the radio blared out. She was in a foul temper – if there was one thing I was aware of, it was my stepmother's moods. I waited for her next move towards me. It came soon enough.

She had got dressed and was about to take the blankets down to the back green to hang out to dry. However, due to my poor attempts at wringing, water splashed onto her as she picked the basket out of the bath. That was like a red rag to a bull. She thundered along the lobby towards my room, shouting and screaming: 'You little bastard! You nasty little bitch! You did that deliberately, didn't you?' I was terrified and braced myself for what was to come. I was trembling and, in my fear, I completely forgot that I was sitting on the bed when I hadn't been given explicit permission to do so. When Helen charged into my room, she was therefore faced with yet another crime I had committed which would allow her to vent her anger on me.

'You little bastard,' she screamed again. 'Look at the fucking mess you've made! And who told you to sit down anyway? Having a nice fucking layabout, are you?' She grabbed me by the hair and dragged me up the lobby to the bathroom, shouting and screaming all the way. When we got to the bathroom she hissed, 'Over the bath. Get over the bath.' Trembling, silently crying, and bracing myself for what was to come, I bent over the old cast-iron bath, feeling the cold through my threadbare vest. I gripped the curled metal edge of the bath and waited for the first wallop of the leather belt across my back and legs. It came soon enough. The leather slaps rained down, every wallop stinging and biting my flesh as she screamed at me and told me to say over and over, 'I am bad! I deserve to be punished! I am a horrible little girl!' It went on and on until she'd decided that she'd given me enough. When she was finished, she yelled at me to get the job done properly this time and to cut out the tears and petted lip. So I got on with it – wringing and wringing the blankets out, over and over, until she was finally satisfied. I was hurting, cold and hungry but I had been really, really bad so I needed to be punished further.

It was barely morning, but I was already on to the next step of punishment that Helen had ruled necessary for me. 'You will stand there, you ugly little witch, and you will keep your hands by your sides without moving a fucking muscle, or I will know.'

She screwed up her eyes at me behind those huge glasses and added, 'And that'll be your day until your Dad gets home.'

I could feel the welts rising on the skin on the backs of my legs and my back. I was morbidly comforted by the warm glow of my wounds. Beatings always hurt afterwards but not as much as when I received them, and I had got used to that 'after beating' feeling, taking a little comfort in the fact that for now it was over. With my hands by my sides, I surveyed my surroundings and used all the little tricks I had developed to help get me through the hours. I counted the cracks and the tiles. I sang songs in my head – '10 Green Bottles', 'Ye Cannae Shove Yer Grannie aff the Bus' – any song I knew that had lots of verses, and nursery rhymes such as 'Jack and Jill', 'Old King Cole', 'Baa Baa Black Sheep'. I'd do anything to relieve the boredom.

To stop myself from getting numb, I'd step from foot to foot. I'd sometimes stand with one foot on the other. Occasionally, a weevil would work its way out from under the bath and I'd amuse myself as I watched its journey, thinking how lucky it was to have so much freedom. Sometimes I would just close my eyes and listen to all the sounds outside that room: the television, the children playing in the back greens below me, dogs barking and gulls calling. Then I'd be making plans for the things I would do when I finally got away from there. Sometimes I took a risk by going to the toilet because, even though I stood there all day, I was not allowed to use it until I was told to by Helen. Most of the time it was just her in the living room as the boys were out all day.

My only break came from stepping into the lobby every now and again when someone came to use the toilet, and sneaking a mouthful of water from the cold tap when I thought it was safe to do so. That was tricky because I couldn't allow there to be one bit of noise or mess. I would put my mouth right over the cold tap and turn it on very slowly and swallow back a mouthful, and then I'd resume my usual stance. Once I was caught right in the act. Helen sneaked up on me while I had my mouth over the tap, standing on my tiptoes. I thought I'd been so clever, that she was still in the living room. Just as I was about to swallow that delicious mouthful of cold water, a hand came whacking on to the back of my head and my teeth clattered against the tap. I felt them cutting through my lip and the water rushing up my nose as I choked and yelped all at once. My heart was racing and I was terrified. I waited for the onslaught, for the beating, for what was going to come next, but that time she didn't do anything more. 'Bed!' she shouted. 'Hands by your side!' I couldn't make sense of that either – this wasn't a punishment; this was luxury compared to standing all day. I was suspicious but just glad to have got away so lightly.

On the day of my punishment for not wringing out the blankets properly, I stood in the cold bathroom all day, from just after breakfast time. I heard the boys come home for something to eat at lunchtime then go out to play again. Later, I heard them coming back in for their tea, and then each of them wanted to use the toilet. I stepped out to let them in.

Then I was given some scraps of tea by Helen's eldest – the boy who had grown from that baby I used to watch her cuddle when she visited me in Barnardo's. He opened the door and put my plate and fork on the floor in front of me before saying, 'You've to leave the plate outside the door, pissy pants.' He shut the door and left, laughing at me. As I stood there, devouring every pathetic morsel on that plate, I could hear them all having tea and giggling and the telly in the background. Today I was on 'half rations' due to me being bad. This surprised me because normally when I was so bad, I'd get no food at all. But, that day, I was fed one slice of chopped pork, a few strands of spaghetti and a couple of chips. I licked the plate clean, put it outside the door as I was told then waited to see what would happen to me next.

After tea, one of the boys came and got the plate, and then they went back out to play as it was still summer. It must have been just after six o'clock when my Dad came home, as I'd heard the opening music of the six o'clock news on television just before I heard the key in the lock. Fortunately, the bathroom wasn't as cold as it was in winter but I was still cold after standing there, hardly moving, all day. As the front door opened, the torture for me was the sun shining down the lobby, and the sound of children playing out in the street. Why couldn't I be one of those normal kids who got to spend the long summer days playing rounders and hopscotch or skipping in the street? What was wrong with me?

I heard my Dad's footsteps coming up the bare floorboards of the lobby. As I listened, my heart raced with fear. I heard him putting his postbag in the cupboard halfway up the hallway. Through the frosted glass window of the bathroom door I watched his shape getting larger as he came nearer, then I watched it disappear as he went into the living room, the television becoming momentarily louder as he opened the door. I heard the kettle whistling for his ritual cup of tea and I heard their voices. It was, at first, just a muffled sound but then Helen's voice got louder and louder as she screamed at my Dad about me. I heard my name being yelled out over and over again. I thought how strange it was that she only called me by my name when she was talking *about* me and never *to* me.

This argument was much the same as any I'd overheard while sitting in my bedroom and listening to every word. My bedroom was more of a boxroom than a bedroom, and its layout made it easy for me to listen in. Helen went on about how I was always being bad; how I wouldn't do as I was told; how I was cheeky to her. She said that she was at breaking point, and that her sons were missing out on things because she had all this extra work with me. I was lazy; I was insolent; I stole food and I wet the bed. All more work for her; all more work for poor, put-upon Helen. It always followed a pattern. After she had ranted, she would ask my Dad what he was going to do about me as she would claim she was at the end of her tether. I'd hear her say, 'I'm trying to be a good mum but she hates me!' and wondered how she could speak that way without the words choking her.

This argument went on, as it always did, until finally I heard my Dad come out of the living room. I could tell by his footsteps that he was angry. He didn't come to the bathroom door as I'd expected, but went charging down the lobby and then stopped two-thirds of the way down. I could see his shape moving around. Then I heard him lifting the hatch to the cellar that ran below our flat, and joined up with a network of cellars that belonged to the various shops and restaurants on Easter Road, all separated by locked wooden doors. I heard him switch on the light he'd installed as he moved the wooden ladder into place that allowed people to go down there.

Then he came to the bathroom.

I bristled with fear as he yanked open the door. I looked up at him standing there in his Post Office trousers with a V-neck sweater over a white shirt and his tie loosened slightly. His eyes were massive brown pools behind NHS glasses. He was angry. I motioned to speak but he yelled at me not to say a word, and said that I was to get down in the cellar and wait for him.

I scurried down the corridor in my bare feet and vest and pants, almost numb from standing in the cold all day. As I passed the living room I caught sight of Helen standing behind the door, watching and listening. I'll never forget that sneer on her face.

I reached the hatch of the cellar and lowered myself onto the wooden ladder that wobbled as I climbed down it. I hated that cellar with its musty smell, cobwebs, dark shadows and cold, deathly feel. I just stood there again – awaiting my fate. I heard the footsteps of both my Dad and Helen walking about, and the muffled sounds of their resumed arguing. Then I heard him coming down the lobby. I watched as his shape occluded the hatch and he descended step by step, getting bigger as he got closer. I felt as if my heart was going to jump out of my chest. I was terrified.

I knew that I was going to get another beating but I just didn't want my Daddy to do it.

He finally got down to where I was, and I stared at the ground, stared at his feet. As I did, he removed the slipper from his right foot and stood with one slipper and one sock-covered foot. He grabbed me and sort of put me over his knee, although I wasn't lying down completely. He started whacking me. Over and over again I was thrashed – combined with what Helen had done to me earlier that day, it was a miracle that my skinny, beaten, malnourished body didn't just give in. All the time that he hit me, my Dad's breathing was laboured.

I tried to tell him to stop. I whimpered at him more than anything, but he just kept hitting and hitting me across the bottom and backs of my legs. He was really angry with me and told me I had to be good. He asked, 'Do you want your mother to leave us all?' My heart screamed out, 'Yes! Yes, I do! I want that woman who is not my mother, who will never be my mother and who says she hates me, to go away for ever. And I want you to look after me, Daddy, to protect me.' But my heart couldn't speak and, in a desperate fit of self-preservation, I said that I wanted her to stay.

The beating continued for a bit longer. My Dad then told me to get to bed and said he didn't want to come home the next day to find out that I'd caused more trouble for my 'Mummy'. I couldn't speak for crying, and I was hurting inside and out. I did what he said and climbed the ladder and went straight into my room. In bed, I did what I did most times after one of these episodes and curled up into a ball under the covers, hugging myself tightly while sobbing as silently as I could.

What surprises me now about this incident, looking back, is that my Dad seemed to think it was normal for his young daughter to be standing in the bathroom in her underwear. I can't understand why he didn't seek to question the bruises that covered the tops of my legs from the beating I'd had in the morning. I would so like to ask him about that now. How could he justify it? No child is ever naughty enough to warrant this kind of punishment, this cruelty. Where was the fatherly hug and the 'how was your day?' Where was the bedtime story, and who was this man who thought I was being treated appropriately? What was happening? How could it be getting even worse? Helen kept saying that I was truly bad. Maybe I was. I felt bad, as if I had done something very evil. I just didn't know what.

I had no Mummy and I was losing my Daddy.

Chapter Eight

༳

An Invitation to a
Party . . .

HELEN'S PARTIES STARTED a little while after Frances and Simon
came home from Barnardo's. My Dad was working many hours
a day by then. I knew about the parties largely because they
started during a summer holiday period from school, and
continued at that time of year until Helen left. She may well have
also hosted them during the day when we were all at school – and
I suspect she did – but I can't know for certain. All I do know is
that during the holidays there would be a party every other day.

Every day Helen had one of her parties was another day
stolen from my childhood.

I was usually the only child in the house during these parties.
The others would all be out, with my big half-sister in charge,
either at the swing park, the play scheme or a holiday club at the
Regent cinema on Abbeymount. I was allowed out to these places
once or twice but certainly not as a rule. I'd be the only one left
behind, as Helen would be punishing me for something.

I dreaded them all going out the door and it closing behind
them – because I knew then what would be coming.

After I wrote my first book, *The Step Child*, there were many
features and interviews in the national press and magazines. A
Scottish newspaper printed a photograph I had never seen before.

That photograph chilled me to the bone. It showed my older half-brother and half-sister with Helen's two boys at the Regent cinema in the late 1960s. It is a publicity shot, where the manager of the cinema is being presented with something by someone else. I've no idea who the two men are, or what this presentation is about, but Helen's youngest boy is sitting on the knee of one of the men, with my older half-sister standing directly behind him, smiling. On the left of the picture is my older half-brother; he, too, is smiling. There are many other children in the picture and they are all happy. They were all there, my half-siblings, but I am not. I know I'm not because I would have remembered such an event. So where was I? It must have been a school holiday, I guess, so that means I would be where I always was. I'd be at home in my usual place, either in the bathroom or my dark boxroom awaiting my fate while Helen entertained her friends. I was part of that entertainment.

Since Helen's trial I have questioned the motives behind her gruesome abuse of me. I have had to try and make sense of what actually happened to me. I wonder if you will understand when I say that, even at her trial, I was still accepting the abuse. I didn't look beyond the fact that I had been abused. I didn't look for her motives or those of her so-called friends. I suppose in some ways I was still conditioned; I was still fearful of her. Standing in the High Court in Edinburgh that day in October 2003, I was still that frightened little girl inside. When I looked at her, as I was instructed to by Lord Hardie to identify her, she had the power to instil an incredible fear in me, even though I was 45 years old.

I was perplexed by the charges laid against her: 'procuring a minor'. I stood in that court back then and really, honestly, didn't understand what had gone on in my childhood. I knew it was wrong – that's why I was there, to get some justice at last – but I had no idea of the whole picture. What has come to light since that day is that I was not the only one she abused; it is not my place to say who that other person was, but there definitely was another person who, like me, was a child at the time. I know this because I have heard their story too. I do not know for sure if there were other children who suffered the same fate as we did, but I do have my suspicions. I can recall an instance at one of those parties when I heard a young girl cry out in pain in the room next to me. I don't know who the girl was or what was being done to her, but I could guess because I recognised the painful, pitiful sobs that were the same as mine.

Helen's parties were really nothing more than a sordid, sick bunch of paedophiles gathering together to exploit a child, a child held captive and provided by Helen to be used and abused by these warped, twisted people. That's what I understand now.

I love parties in my life today because we have healthy, happy family get-togethers where we enjoy each other's company. We listen to music, eat food and laugh and joke. Any children who are at these parties are respected and protected, an integral part of happy celebrations. It is a far, far cry from the parties I knew as a child where I would be fearful of every sound, where I was far from respected and protected. In complete contrast to a day being stolen, our parties today are days to be treasured, and the memories of them are happy and wholesome. I wonder if Helen Ford can say the same?

༃

Chapter Nine

THE DARLING OF ALL

WHEN I ORIGINALLY DECIDED to tell my story, I didn't know what I wanted from it. This far down the line, however, I can see the huge benefit I have gained from just being able to get everything out. Before I did this, I wanted to bottle everything up. I really didn't think anyone would believe me if I told them; furthermore, it was just too painful to think about.

During the court case against Helen, she and her 'friends' appeared to be the only guilty ones, but when I look at my father's role in my upbringing I see that he, too, is accountable. I also see that I was badly let down by all the organisations involved in my childhood, from the social workers who visited every four to six weeks – some of whom recognised something was wrong but did nothing – to the schools I attended where teachers saw a steady decline in my behaviour and witnessed my bruises, yet did nothing.

It seems incredible to me now, as an adult, that I was actually taken to be assessed by doctors after I was caught stealing at school. The files I have report that I was stealing food at home and from children's bags and pockets at school. That was perfectly true – I took food from any source I could. I'd pick half-eaten sweets from the pavements, and eat bread thrown out for the birds. I'd even steal food from bins. I was starving. I needed to eat. I'd go to school hungry having had no breakfast and possibly no tea or half rations the previous night. I was stopped from having school dinners by Helen and made to come home at lunchtime each day so that she could maintain control. It was hardly surprising that I stole food.

As I pointed out at Helen's trial, the only child who feels the need to do that is a hungry child. It was a cry for help, not naughtiness. So, at one stage, I was referred to a child psychologist because my stepmother said she was at the end of her tether with my behaviour.

I have since questioned why Helen said there was a problem with my behaviour. She was treating me so badly, so cruelly, that it seems unbelievable that she would be the one to actually draw attention to how I was behaving. I think that, by this stage, she was so confident of two things that she simply didn't think she would be caught. Her first line of defence would have been the impression she gave everyone of being the perfect wife and mother. She was the young woman who had taken on all these kids who weren't her own or even, in the case of my two half-siblings, her husband's. Even when she had two little ones of her own she kept everything together. The second thing was that she was fully aware of what an arch manipulator she was. She was skilled at getting people to think what she wanted, and she probably would have assumed she could talk her way out of anything. I also think she was probably covering her own back – if she could get me labelled as a problem child, then anything I might say about her wouldn't stick.

Unlike many of my other memories – where there is nothing on paper to back up that *I do* remember things accurately, *I do* know what went on – I have some social work files from this time. In them are various comments relating directly to the reasons for me going to the Children's Psychology Department in Rillbank Terrace (a child and adolescent mental health unit) in

Edinburgh in the first place, and what was recorded after my visits there. In the report of 20 December 1968, the files say:

> *On the way to the door Mother said that Donna was really the trouble maker because she was 'stealing food at all hours'. Mrs Ford said things would be much better if Donna wasn't there.*

The outcome of this was that it was recommended I see a psychologist. This strikes me as rather odd – my stepmother says that I am stealing food and I'm almost immediately sent to a psychologist? Perhaps things just worked differently in the 1960s, but I doubt that state-funded psychologists were readily on hand to provide support for one comment made about a child. Perhaps there are other files that say other things, but I wonder whether someone, somewhere, had already had their suspicions aroused about Helen, and decided to keep an eye on things by making me attend Rillbank regularly. What I do know is that I was then taken there on a weekly basis by either my Dad or Helen. In a report dated 5 August 1969, a psychiatrist from the Royal Hospital for Sick Children in Edinburgh states:

> *Donna is very unhappy and isolated. She suffers from a behaviour disorder which causes her to steal from school and from home.*

She suggests regular psychotherapy. Whether anything was done to delve into *why* a 10-year-old girl was so unhappy and had feelings of isolation, I have no idea. Given what my life was like, and how it was about to continue, I guess not. Six months later, on 2 February 1970, another comment in the files says:

> *Miss H rang Miss B of Rillbank who agreed to visit. Said she found difficulty in making a relationship with Mrs Ford who*

adopted an aggressive attitude. The father is much more
reasonable.

So, there were concerns. People had noticed what Helen was like, but – even after she left – no-one seemed to see the need to get to the root of it all. In a later visit of 24 April 1972, after Helen had left, the files show that I was truanting a lot and there was concern over this. The social worker, Miss J K, suggested that the school refer me to an educational psychologist. My father's reply was, 'Well, she used to see a psychiatrist, but then Mrs Ford went and stopped that.' I do not know why she stopped the visits but I do know that they stopped as quickly as they started. In one report, which has no date, my father is quoted as saying, 'Mrs Ford felt very embarrassed at having to take her to the psychiatrist.'

These files are the only means I have of trying to fill in the blank spaces in my memory and explaining the things I missed as a child, because I only saw what Helen and my Dad allowed me to see. I feel in many ways – even other than the obvious – I was made a scapegoat by Helen. By this time, she was pregnant with her third baby, so the question of me seeing a psychologist came at a difficult time when she would have known that the baby was not my father's. Focusing the attention on me may well have deflected it from her.

⁓

At the start of the files I have (from 6 January 1961), I am described as 'a happy child full of life'. At just over 18 months, when I was admitted to the care of Barnardo's, I was described as a responsive, placid child with a happy smile who got on with everyone. To give them credit, they seemed to have kept me that way. When I was 'restored' to the care of my Dad and Helen on 8 July 1964, I was five years, one month and two days old. My character at that time was described as, 'Good. An affectionate child.' Alongside some comments about my half-siblings, the report continues: 'Little Donna is especially charming . . . she has not yet started school but is a bright wee girl . . . the darling of all.' I am further described as clean, healthy, affectionate and polite.

Once I had been taken back to Edinburgh, the reports do raise a few concerns. Given that these official documents are often full of careful wording, I think that it is still relatively easy to hear the worried phrases which are there. By 8 June 1970 the social worker reports on a home visit:

> *I found Mrs Ford and the children all at home. One child G* [Helen's eldest] *was playing outside all the others were sitting in the kitchen watching television. Mrs F was resplendent in a gold blouse and yellow trousers. Donna is very small for her age and I felt there was a 'cowed' look about her or maybe she is just shy. She was 'cleaning up' another room when I arrived.*

I know that, on this occasion, Helen had forgotten that the social worker was due to visit and, as usual, I had been sent to my room as soon as I returned from school. I was a very frightened, abused little girl and this report in particular is the most poignant because it was at the end of this year that the worst abuse of my life occurred. Why did this social worker not investigate her suspicions further? Other entries in this report point to further concerns such as: 'Neither of the girls [my elder half-sister and I] nor A [my elder half-brother] was dressed nicely. There is a marked difference between the Ford children and the other three.' A marked difference indeed.

Chapter Ten

৵

'HAPPY NORMAL CHILDREN'

AS AN ADULT, READING THROUGH these files makes me so angry. Vital warning signals were not picked up on. I was a little girl who was being abused. My older siblings were also 'at risk'. But although these signs were noted, they were ultimately dismissed and overlooked.

On 5 March 1965, just before they were 'restored' to the care of my Dad and Helen, my elder half-brother and half-sister were both reported as being 'happy normal children'. By December 1966, these children had also changed. The police called at my father's workplace to return the two of them as they had run away from Edina Place during the night. Of this incident the files say, 'They had slipped out of the house during the night after being punished by their father and Mrs Ford.' I recall clearly the events leading up to that incident and what happened afterwards.

Helen had given birth to another son, Andrew, in November 1966, and it was clear by then that she was unable to cope with all the responsibility she had. We were all unhappy as we were being beaten and punished on a regular basis, so, after all being hit really badly again one night, the three of us hatched a plan to run away together. I soon chickened out – being the youngest I was too scared to go with them – but they decided to go it alone.

The next morning, Helen came into my bedroom first thing and obviously knew that the others had gone. 'Where are they?' she asked, shaking me into a sitting position and grabbing my arms. 'Where have those other two little bastards gone?' I was bleary-eyed and still sore from the beating of the previous evening. 'I don't know where they are!' I said, and I was telling the truth. The plan we had all concocted was half-baked and, if the others had come up with any detailed escape route, they wouldn't have told me anyway as I was too little in their eyes. 'Don't you lie to me,' Helen shouted. 'You're all in this together, all you little bastards!' She went on and on with her usual tirade, name-calling and hysteria. Naturally, it became physical and she tried to, as she said, 'beat it out of me'. There was no point in her trying, as I didn't know anything, but that didn't stop her.

Later that day, my Dad came home with the two runaways. The police had gone to the GPO where he worked, after finding the children at St Andrew Square bus station trying – in vain – to get away somewhere. Anywhere, I'd guess. My Dad explained all of this to Helen and then went back to work. He had barely left the house when she started on us. Although most of her physical and verbal anger was concentrated on the two older children, she hissed to me that, 'You needn't think I've forgotten about you.'

All of us were set to scrubbing the house, but she dragged me off cleaning duties at one point as she said that I wasn't 'putting my back into it'. Off I was sent to the bathroom and made to stand over the bath, as usual, while she beat me with a belt. I was calling out, 'No, Mummy! No, Mummy! I promise I'll be good, Mummy!' but this seemed to enrage her still further. Whacking at me even more, she shouted, 'I'm not your Mummy! How often do I have to tell you that I'm not your Mummy? You have no Mummy, you little bastard, and you will call me Mrs Ford if you know what's good for you!'

ॐ

From an early age, we had been brought to the attention of the RSPCC, and from that moment there were files on all of us. There were files from Barnardo's, Social Work Department files, files from Rillbank, doctors' files and school files. Each one of them expressed a concern, yet nothing was done. When these files were produced in the High Court in Edinburgh in 2003, they showed a pattern and a link of opinions that was not picked up on and recognised back in the days when I was left there to my fate.

As an adult I asked my father why he had let things go on. He just turned his head away, without giving me so much as one word for an answer. Why did he do nothing? Why did he not see what she was doing? How could he be so blind? What made him take her word without even asking me? Fathers are supposed to be protectors. They are supposed to love us and nurture us and listen to us and allow us a voice. They are supposed to praise us and instil us with confidence. My father didn't do any of these things. Yes, he gave me a roof over my head, but it was never a home.

How I craved the same attention that he gave his boys with Helen, who were both golden in hair and nature in his eyes, as that was what she told him and that was what he chose to believe. Never once did he see or question my bruises or gaunt appearance, nor did he notice the vacant look I knew I wore when I had been sexually abused.

I felt different after the sexual abuse began. I knew that I acted differently too because I couldn't bear to look at people. I was too embarrassed. I was mortified about what had happened to me, what had been done to me. I didn't really know very much about what had gone on, but I knew it was wrong. That my own Daddy wouldn't notice seems beyond neglect.

My father would come back from work and know only what Helen told him. He may have been tired from work and life but he never noticed me full stop. Even when he had to reprimand me he did it without really looking at me. Did he just switch off? Did he believe what Helen told him, that I was bad? Or did he just not care?

I have very mixed feelings about my Dad. I always wanted his love and approval but I thought he was a weak man. He was controlled by Helen when she lived with him, then when she left, he was controlled by drink. Was he an alcoholic? I don't know. He claimed that he went out to the pub because he needed adult conversation; he claimed he needed a drink to relax him. He didn't go a day without a drink so I would say that he was definitely dependent on drink, and if being dependent on drink deems you an alcoholic then, yes, that's what he was.

᠀

When I was a little girl, I wished that someone would come in and save me, take me away somewhere nice, look after me and love me for ever. It never happened. When I was older, looking back, I wished that someone would just hold my hand and go back in there with me and stop me being scared. I want people to know how bad it was because it happens to so many children, and it shouldn't.

This genre of books has been widely criticised for its value or purpose. However, writing my story has been a saviour for me. It wouldn't work for me to talk about what went on with a stranger. I have worked things through in my own way because that is right for me. I know there are many wonderful organisations out there that offer excellent counselling services, and people must look at all of their options and choose what is right. For me, though, writing is my method of healing. I write the memory down, and by doing that I am able to think about what went on, and I am able to see that I am away from all that now. I can apportion blame where blame is due. I can look at how it has affected me personally, and ultimately I can move on.

And moving on is something I want to do so very badly.

༂

Chapter Eleven

Nellie and Madge

AUNTIE NELLIE WOULD BE SO proud of me, I just know she would.

Auntie Nellie was my Dad's aunt, technically my great-aunt, a title befitting such a magnificent lady. In *The Step Child* I told the story of Auntie Nellie and how she was my greatest influence back then, the only light in some very dark days. I still sometimes comfort myself with memories of how she would take me out once a month to Jenners for high tea, and to Marks and Spencer's to buy me school uniforms. Nellie had been a headmistress and was a fine, gentle, elegant, well-travelled lady. She introduced me to books and education – she was the greatest inspiration of my life.

I lost her through no fault of my own when Gordon made me steal her purse and put all of the blame on me. Nellie couldn't forgive that because, for her, stealing was such a heinous crime. She died without knowing the truth about what really went on, but I have never forgotten her and her teachings. I carry her with me always.

༂

Many of the women I admire and respect in my adult life have an element of Auntie Nellie in them; they are sophisticated, cultured and unmistakably good people. It may seem odd that Helen allowed me the privilege of contact with Auntie Nellie, but she did it for one reason and one reason alone – the reason that was always most important to her – money. Auntie Nellie had a house in the Colinton district, a smart Edinburgh suburb. She had plenty of money and would be leaving it as an inheritance to someone. Helen probably assumed that it would be left to me as Nellie was always fond of me. She also no doubt assumed that I wouldn't see a penny of it, as she and my Dad would have full access to it. However, Helen didn't want to leave anything to chance, so she usually sent her eldest son, Gordon, with me when I went to visit. Presumably, she thought she was covering all bases, and that Nellie would become fond of Gordon too, and leave money to both of us. Only a mother could be so blind. Helen had turned Gordon into an obnoxious, loathsome, cruel little liar – and exactly the sort of child Nellie would never fall for.

One thing Helen had done well in terms of her mothering was to raise that boy to be nasty – because of that, my stepmother never saw the colour of Nellie's money when she died. Back then, when I was chastised and beaten for blowing this golden opportunity for her, I was saddened – not by the loss of money, but for the loss of such a wonderful person in my life. What I didn't see then was that, actually, Auntie Nellie *had* left me an inheritance, and it was far greater than money could ever buy.

I had the gift of goodness bestowed upon me through this lovely woman. I also benefited in far greater a way than Helen would ever have known, and that was through the books that Auntie Nellie had left for my Dad.

These books were kept in the boys' room, which had an adjoining door into my bedroom (originally the boxroom). My bed ran alongside this door, and on the other side of it was my elder half-brother's bed. I knew about these books that Auntie Nellie had left because I was given the job of putting them away in the press. As I put them away, I hatched a plan to sneak some into my room. I had to wait until there was enough noise in the living room, usually when they were all having tea, then I'd open the door just enough so that I could squeeze through. Then I'd quickly – and as quietly as I could – get the book I'd earmarked and sneak it back into my room, putting it under my mattress. The whole time my heart would be racing with the fear of getting caught and also with the excitement of managing to get one over on Helen.

These books saved me because they offered me an escape. When people talk about never underestimating the power of the written word, I feel that I am a living example of that. I learned so much through books as a child. Mostly I read novels – *Little Women, What Katy Did, Oliver Twist, David Copperfield* – but sometimes I would be so scared of being caught that I'd grab the first one that came to hand. Occasionally, I'd end up with a gardening book, and once I got Patrick Moore's *Sky at Night*! No matter what book I got, I read it, or sometimes I just looked at the pictures. Now and again I would use the plain piece of paper at the front of these books to do little drawings, usually of the story I was reading. I suppose it is because of my love of books and the importance they played in my childhood that it seemed the most natural progression in the world for me to write a book and tell my own story.

I often wonder why Helen kept these books. I can't remember her reading much herself. Most of these books from Auntie Nellie were classics, the kind you would expect a retired teacher like her to have. The light was poor in my bedroom but I always managed to get a chink of it somewhere, usually by the door. When I felt it was safe, I would crouch down by the door, holding the book to the light, and I'd read and read. All the time, I'd be listening and watching for someone coming. If someone did come, I'd have to quickly run and put the book under my mattress and get back into my 'position' – hands by my sides, sitting upright in bed or standing with my face against the wall. Through these books, I educated myself and obtained hope. I gained a very different perspective on life from the one I was personally experiencing.

For many years, losing Auntie Nellie was a great source of pain. I couldn't recall the memories of her without hurting. Now, however, with the freedom I have achieved from bringing all the dark horrible things that went on into the light, I can also enjoy the memories of Auntie Nellie. I no longer blame myself for losing her as I did back then, and I can look back on what she gave me rather than what I lost. The same can be said of my Dad's sister, Auntie Madge. For years, I mistrusted her because she was friendly with Helen, but when I look back now I realise that she, too, in her way, was also giving me something.

Auntie Madge was the baby of the family, the only girl among three brothers. She was unmarried – a spinster, as they called any woman who was unmarried in those days. A small lady, she wore glasses and looked a lot like my Dad. She was always immaculately groomed with neatly coiffed hair and smart Jackie Kennedy style clothes. Her shoes and bags were always matching, and she wore gloves and a hat. She worked as a secretary and was quite independent.

My earliest memories of her are in the flat in Easter Road. I remember one occasion when she visited and I was sitting upright in the bunk bed in my vest and pants with my hands by my sides. I don't know why I was there, but I must have been 'bad' and on a punishment. What I recall is Auntie Madge coming through and reading me a story. This was a revelation as nobody ever read me stories.

Then there were times later on in my life, after Helen left, when Madge invited me up to her smart new house in Murrayburn, a new housing scheme, and tried to teach me about grooming. I can see that little house now in my mind. It was so smart and clean with flowery curtains and a soft sofa. The radiogram would be playing 'Telstar' by the Tornados; she loved her music, the Shadows being a particular favourite. We'd sit on her sofa and she'd show me how to do my nails, how to file them and buff them before applying clear polish. She lathered Pond's cold cream on her face every day and Pond's vanishing cream once a week. Auntie Madge, like Auntie Nellie, was a million miles away from the only woman I had known – Helen.

I would have liked to have found out more about Madge. I wish I could have sat down and talked to her about her family, about how she and my Dad and their brothers grew up, but sadly she died when I was in my twenties. The last thing I heard about her was that she had crippling arthritis and was on gold injections to relieve the symptoms. I didn't really know her that well – I didn't see her every week or anything like that – but what I did know of her left an impression on me. She was independent at a time when a big question mark hung over the head of any woman who was not married in their twenties; she was self-sufficient and a respectable, kind woman; and she was my Dad's sister. I wish she had seen something in me that might have made her want to help.

꙳

Granny Ford was the mother of Auntie Madge and my Dad. She was also a positive influence for me, even though my memories of her are even fewer and sketchier. I can look back and see us visiting her in her little cottage in Ashley Terrace. I'd play in her garden while she cooked mince and tatties, and I'd hear the ticking sounds of the cuckoo clock that my Dad brought back from Germany when he was in the army.

She had neat grey hair, curled and pinned, and her pinny was always tied around her waist. She hugged me and sang to me.

When I was around eight and still in the flat in Easter Road, she died. My Dad was bereft. It was the only time I ever saw him cry. Apparently, Granny Ford fell in her bathroom, having suffered a stroke, and bumped her head, causing her death. I didn't go to the funeral as children just didn't go to them in those days. She, like Auntie Nellie, just left my life.

゛゛

Auntie Nellie was a good person. Auntie Madge was a good person, and my memories of my Dad's mum – Granny Ford – are also good. These are the important things to me. They were my Dad's family and they were good and kind people. I had small glimpses of this kindness and goodness in my Dad in the very early days, and I know that Karen – Helen's youngest child – saw a goodness in him too. With all this knowledge I am able to see that possibly, without the influence of Helen in his life, he was like his family – basically decent. However, he was also a misguided person who was heavily influenced by Helen's evil. It is heartening for me to know that my side of the family is that way.

I can't say the same for Helen.

My birth mother and her family don't come into it because they don't really care – if they did they would have found me long before now. I shudder to think what would have happened to me if I hadn't had the influence of these people in my terrible childhood. I am eternally grateful to Auntie Nellie, Auntie Madge and Granny Ford for giving me some of their goodness in those terrible dark painful days. These are the important legacies, the legacies I can hand on to my children – not the twisted, perverse ways of Helen and her paedophile friends, and certainly not the legacy of a mother who abandoned me when I was just a baby.

᠍

ERRANDS

I DON'T KNOW HOW the minds of other people work. Do they have flashes of memories coming through when they least expect or want them? I do. Especially now. Since the court case, since I faced Helen Ford and watched as she was found guilty, then sentenced, more and more is coming through and forcing me to look at what happened to me. I don't go for counselling. I don't have a team of psychiatrists and psychologists there to help me through every thought. I really only have myself.

How can I know everything that was done to me? No-one remembers every single day of their childhood. Even when that childhood is filled with horror, there are ordinary days and times when life just goes on. But then, of course, come the things that no-one ever wants to think about. There are many episodes of my abuse that I have only glimpsed fleetingly – I assume that the power of my mind blocks things that are too awful, or prevents too many incidents being relived at once.

I remember Blind Jimmy. I remember the stench of the old man I was sent to 'help'. He was a disgusting creature with never a nice word to say to anyone, and on the day Helen sent me to him to 'help', I was horrified just to think I would have to clean and tidy up for him, horrified to even spend any time in that filthy grey flat. I should have known. Looking back, when he started to abuse me – holding my hand to masturbate him while he stuck his fingers into me, laughing and wheezing all the time – it was almost to be expected.

I remember the barber. I remember the red-and-white striped pole and the bowl of sweeties for kids who got their hair cut by him. Helen sent me to him with a note – and a warning not to read it. As with Blind Jimmy, as with all of my abusers, Helen didn't just know what was going to happen; she facilitated it. As I sat on the swirling barber shop chair – enjoying the sights flying past, enjoying *fun* for once – Helen would have known why the barber locked the door after reading her note, why he smiled at me in a different way to any other time, why he pulled the blinds down, why he felt it would be absolutely danger-free to stick his hands up my skirt, and force them inside me.

She also sent me to the homes of men she considered 'friends'. I remember some of those instances clearly. Too clearly.

There was always a created reason behind these trips. I do wonder why. Everyone involved seemed to be so sure of themselves, as if they would never have to account for their actions. Yet there was always a pretence, whether it was a note, a chore or an errand. One day during the summer holidays when we were living in Edina Place, I was given one of the dreaded folded-up notes.

'You!' Helen screamed from the kitchen through to me in my dark little bedroom. I'd been hoping that she'd forget about me and that the worst thing I'd have to deal with that day would be boredom. As soon as I heard her voice, however, I knew that was a pipe dream.

I scrambled off my bed, hiding the book I'd been trying to read in the mattress hole where I kept my treasured fiction from Auntie Nellie. I scurried through to the kitchen where Helen stood, holding a wet tea towel in one hand and a bit of paper in the other. Every word that came from her mouth was accompanied by a slap of the tea towel at my face and head: 'Take – this – and – get – across – the – road.' I took the note and left the room. 'Don't you dare fucking read that, witch!' she shouted at me, as always.

I ran out of the door and across to the flat in Easter Road where I knew a man (whom I'll call Johnny Smith) lived. The whole community around that area at the time knew most people – if not by name, then by sight – because everyone could get pretty much everything they needed in terms of shopping and services without ever leaving the area. There were a lot of people with small minds and no ambition who would never go beyond Easter Road for their entire lives. I knew that Mr Smith was a friend of Helen's. Even though I had never seen him at any of her parties, she always spoke to him if she bumped into him when we were shopping, and their conversations left her in a good mood as the pair of them enjoyed a laugh when they met.

I walked over to where the tenement flats were and opened the heavy door which led into the stone stairwell. The note was probably about a party Helen was planning, I reasoned. There was a feeling of dread in my stomach as I didn't know whether it would be the next day or next week, but I knew that I would be part of the 'entertainment' whenever it did happen. I went up the stairs to the second-floor flat which I knew belonged to Mr Smith. He must have been waiting for me because he opened the door before I'd even managed to ring the bell.

'Come in, come in,' he said, pulling me by the wrist into his flat. He had horrible teeth – more gums than anything else – and he smelled as though he didn't even know what a bath was. Helen didn't keep me clean, and I was never allowed free access to the bathroom to wash myself (that was a place for punishment), but I seemed to have a heightened sensitivity to the stink of others too. He started to pull me through to what must have been his living room. 'I have to go,' I stuttered. 'I have to get back or Helen will wonder where I am.' I'd tried that line many times before with many of Helen's friends, and it had never worked. It wasn't to be any different today. All of these men knew – as did I – that Helen had sent me to them. Helen couldn't care less what they did to me once I was in their homes or shops.

'No, no,' he answered. 'Don't you worry about that, Donna. Helen says you can stay here as long as you like.' I didn't 'like' to stay there for another second. His attempts to pull me towards the living room were becoming more successful. When we got there, he pushed me down onto an old, smelly easy chair and leaned over me. 'Now, Donna, can I get you anything?' he asked, as if we were having a perfectly normal conversation. I wanted lots of things – mostly an escape route out of there. I shook my head. 'Ah well, now – maybe I'll be able to think of something,' he leered.

He stood up and moved his hand towards the front of his trousers. As soon as he started to unzip them, I made a dash for it, pushing past him and running down the hall. I heard him coming along behind me, calling my name in an almost sing-song way, as I finally got to the safety of the front door.

The locked front door.

He put his arms above me as I stood there. 'See? See what a silly wee girl you are?' he asked. He moved his hands down, grabbing me by the shoulders. I closed my eyes, but he told me to open them. 'Don't you want to, Donna?' he said. 'Don't you want to lick my lollipop?'

He stood there smiling with his trousers and pants around his feet, and shoved my hand onto his horrible, inflated penis. 'There you go,' he said. 'I knew you'd like it. Now, go ahead – lick my lollipop.' He kept saying it over and over again, more to himself than to me I think, as he pushed my head down and forced me to do what he wanted.

Finally, it was over. That scene – that moment – was over at least, but it's only very recently that my memory has allowed me to visit that chapter again. I know that there are many, many more episodes all too similar to that one, still locked away. Whether they will come out – when they will come out – isn't something I have any control over, but maybe you are only given what you can cope with. I hope so.

Chapter Thirteen

✂

SUFFER THE LITTLE
CHILDREN

ON THE BACK OF MY BIRTH certificate is written, 'baptised at London Road Church, Edinburgh on June 9th 1966 by Rev W Scott Reid'.

I wasn't a baby when that baptism happened, nor was my mother present. In fact, it occurred almost two years after I was 'restored' to the care of my Dad and his new wife Helen.

Reading through my files – particularly those that relate directly to my time in the Barnardo's institution – there is much mention of religion, or the lack of it, within our family. My mother is referred to as a 'lapsed Catholic', and it is stated that, 'the children have not been baptised'. On my return home it was a prerequisite that I would be given a religious education, so, every Sunday without fail, I attended Sunday school. My Dad and Helen didn't go, but my older half-brother and half-sister came with me when they too arrived 'home'.

The memories I have of attending Sunday school are bittersweet. I can recall some nice times such as singing jolly children's hymns. I also loved the Sunday school picnics where, for one day of the year, I would get the opportunity to travel on a bus with all the other kids, and we'd arrive at a park where I could play like a normal child. On top of that, I'd be fed! I'd receive a little paper bag with a cold meat pie, a biscuit and a homemade bun. On those days I was truly in heaven.

At Sunday school I would listen to the Bible stories related to us by our teacher, about the miracles that were performed by a mystical person called Jesus. I didn't know who Jesus was but He sounded good and kind. I loved these stories – the birth of the baby Jesus; the parting of the waves; the Ten Commandments; and how Jesus fed so many people with a few fish and loaves. However, one story that sticks like glue in my mind and seemed terribly apt to me is the verse from Matthew – suffer the little children.

If there is one clear image in my mind, it is the day that I heard these words. I was around nine years old and we had been living in our new house for a matter of months. The week of this sermon was the week that I had, for the first time ever, been sexually abused.

I was sore all over that Sunday morning – bruised on my body from the beating I'd received on one of the days that week, and sore down below because that week I had been sent on an errand to one of Helen's friends. The man I had been sent to had stuck his fingers 'in there'. He told me I would like it, but I didn't, I truly didn't.

That Sunday, I got up and got dressed as I had been instructed by Helen. Wearing the best of the clothes I had, I walked up Easter Road with my half-brother and half-sister. Frances was holding one of my hands, and, in the other, I clutched the round copper penny I had been told to place in the big brass collection plate as it was handed round at the end of the service. Even now, I can feel the tears stinging my eyes as I remember how we walked up that road passing all the familiar shops, most of them closed now.

The stillness of the day was disturbed only by the clanging of the bells leading us all into the big church like ants. When we got there my sister went into the main part of the church where all the adults stayed. I didn't know what she did there, but my brother and I, like all the other children, went into the little room at the side where the Sunday school was held.

We all sat down on mats that were placed haphazardly on the wooden floor. First, we prayed then we sang a song. I don't recall what that song was, but I remember looking at all the other children and wondering why they were so happy. Our Sunday school teacher went on to tell us the story of people bringing their children to Jesus so that he might put his hands on them to bless them. The disciples disagreed with this and Jesus said: 'suffer the little children'. That was it. That was all I heard. Even Jesus – this person whom I thought was a nice man – agreed that children should suffer, that I should suffer.

I was bereft. I didn't hear or understand the next part where the teacher went on to say that innocents such as children should be welcome in the Kingdom of Heaven. All I heard was that it was fine for me to be suffering and that Jesus approved of it. This Sunday school, this place, was the only solace for me in my life. I welcomed my time away from Helen to listen to something nice, but even here – in my eyes – it was okay for the things that were happening to me to happen. Jesus, too, was a man and He thought it was acceptable for children to suffer. At that precise moment in time, I felt that there was no way out for me.

The pain of that moment was terrible. I clutched the penny and wanted to run away with it, but I didn't. I put it into the collection plate when it came round, and I walked home with my sister and brother, hurting even more than when I had set out that morning. That Sunday afternoon, as I lay in my bed in my dark boxroom, listening to 'Sing Something Simple' on the radio, I vowed that I would never ever trust Jesus. Now, as an adult, I have enormous respect for anyone who has a religion and uses it in the correct way, and I understand fully what was meant by the words in this particular chapter of the Bible. But if there ever was an illustration of how easy it is for children to misconstrue words then this must be it.

꒓

The hell at 'home' was being exacerbated by Helen's eldest son, who had learned all he knew from his mother. Gordon was by far the favourite. In her eyes he could do no wrong, whereas in fact he was the most horrible boy ever. He was two years old when I went to live with them, but he was never the sweet little baby brother I'd hoped for. I know as an adult that it wasn't his fault, and that it was the way he was brought up by Helen that made him sneaky and spiteful, but it was really terrible living with him.

Helen made it clear from the word go that he was 'special' and I was not. She constantly sang to him and bounced him on her knee. He was hugged and played with – even my Dad was like this with him. Gordon had his own toys and nice clothes even when money was tight. It is hard for me now to believe that he was three years younger than me because he was to become such a tormenter. By the time he could talk he was encouraged to 'tell on' me. If I was standing somewhere on punishment, he would call to Helen that I had 'moved' and I would be beaten on his word. He would come into the bathroom when I was standing there and shout and scream. When Helen came running, he would say I had hit him and I would be beaten again.

This set the pattern for his daily behaviour. By the time we moved house when I was eight and he was five, Helen wouldn't blink an eye at him kicking me as I stood in punishment. I was powerless to say anything about this; my breath would have been wasted. Gordon would sometimes bring me my food into the bathroom or my bedroom, and he would spit in it first or throw it down so that it spilled all over the floor. He would then laugh at me as I scrambled to scrape up this precious food from the floor with not a shred of dignity left. When Helen left, he was knocked off his pedestal a bit as he could no longer behave like this in front of my father; so he would wait until my Dad wasn't around, then he would start his nipping, kicking and tormenting.

Once, I managed to get him into trouble with my Dad. I was around 13, and Gordon would have been 10. My Dad had been out at the pub as usual, and while he was there Gordon had niggled and niggled at me, calling me a bastard and constantly kicking his football at me. By the time my Dad came back I was in a terrible state, crying as if my heart would break. After hearing what had happened, my Dad whacked his son with a slipper. This was far too much humiliation for Gordon, as not only was my Dad punishing him for the first time ever, but he was doing it in front of me too, the lowest of the low. You may think that this would be balancing – that Gordon would have learned a lesson – but this was not to be.

He waited and finally got his revenge on me. As he always did.

I'm not sure exactly how this incident came about, but he asked me to go with him to a printer's yard halfway down our street where he played football with his friends. I was presumably lulled into a false sense of security by his apparent niceness. I had left Karen in the house with my Dad and I can remember being aware that I must get back to give her some lunch. It was a warm sunny day and the printer's yard was closed – it must have been because we could only play in the grounds when it was closed. I recognised most of the boys as being from the gang that all hung around the street. They were much the same age as Helen's son, except for one boy who was a couple of years older.

I didn't think much of it when they stopped kicking their ball on my approach and the older boy said hello. 'Come roond here and see what we found,' said one to me. 'Aye,' said another, 'come and see.' I didn't sense anything amiss so I went round the corner into a recess that housed some bins, not really knowing what to expect. As we went round into this place, two of the boys grabbed me by the arms as the older boy came towards me. He started touching me, lifting up my skirt and pulling at my pants. I tried to kick out at him, and I was yelling at him to 'Fuck off! Fuck off! Get lost!' I was shouting and screaming, but, before I knew it, I was down on the ground and he was on top of me. I could hear all the other boys laughing and shouting as I lay on the ground with this boy pushed on my body, the gravel digging into my exposed flesh.

Again, I was powerless and helpless.

Again.

I tried to push him off. I tried to fight him but he just pinned me down and started moving on top of me, pushing himself into me. Doing all of the things I hated – and recognised so well.

When he finished, he got off me and I jumped up. Making myself as decent as I could, I ran away from them. As I ran, I could hear their laughter and the fact that they had simply gone back to bouncing the ball off the ground. I have never known whether he was old enough to have any real idea of what was going to happen, or did happen, but as I ran away I caught sight of Helen's boy, Gordon, laughing and laughing as the tears of humiliation and frustration streamed down my face.

అ

The last time I was conscious of this spawn of Helen Ford's was in 2003 at the High Court in Edinburgh. He was a man now and he stood there as a witness for his mother. I was revealing her cruelty and he was defending her, saying what a wonderful mother she was. I know that he is technically my half-brother but I do not class him as anything to do with me. I can accept no link because of the way he was.

He should heed the warning that 'what goes around comes around'.

It was one of the lessons I did heed from Sunday school.

Chapter Fourteen

ప్ర

ANDREW AND KAREN

HELEN'S YOUNGEST BOY WAS THE antithesis of his older brother. Andrew was a meek, mild-mannered child who always wore a cheeky grin on his face. He was born in November 1966 in the house in Easter Road. It was lovely to have a new baby around because quite often I would get the job of pushing him in his pram in the back green to get him to settle. I liked those times because I could pretend that I had a dolly to play with, which I longed for.

Gordon, though, was not as happy to have him around. He was very jealous of this little thing taking his place. No longer was he the one getting all the attention; here was a threat to the affections of his mother. He would often nip baby Andrew or torment him when Helen wasn't looking. When the baby cried, it wouldn't be Gordon who got into trouble; it would be me.

I can't recall having an enormous amount of interaction with Andrew; often, he just went off into his own little world. Yet he must have been so alone and confused in that terrible, dysfunctional house. I have a school photograph of him when he was around 10, a fair-haired, blue-eyed child wearing exactly the expression I recall when I think of him.

Although he was treated differently from me by Helen, I can't ever remember him being really nasty. Yes, he joined in watching brother Gordon taunt me, and he was not discouraged by Helen, but he seemed different. He, too, was a witness for Helen at her trial, but unlike her older son I didn't recognise him as the man he had become. As far as I am concerned, Andrew was another one of Helen's victims. He was only six years old when his mother left him. She also left someone who, to me, was far more precious.

Helen's youngest child was a little girl called Karen, born in October 1969. This baby was to change things dramatically for me. Through her I was to learn how to love someone and to know how it felt to have someone love you back.

The run-up to Karen's birth was a frenetic, fraught time in the house because there were so many arguments between my father and Helen. I can only speculate that this may well have had something to do with the miracle of Helen becoming pregnant when my father knew he could no longer have children. Maybe there were a few discussions over who the biological father could be. I recall the day of her birth clearly and how she was born at home in the bedroom my Dad shared with Helen. I remember Helen's moans and the fuss and drama, then seeing the placenta lying in a potty in the bath.

When I saw Karen, I was so pleased because she was lovely. She was round and cherubic and so vulnerable. I got many opportunities to push her up and down the lobby in her big pram, rocking her to sleep; and as I did, I pretended – as with her brother – that she was my dolly. I'm sure if Helen had realised how much I enjoyed this 'chore', she would have stopped it.

I was so small that I could push the pram by going under the handle and moving it from the end of the pram itself. As I pushed and rocked her, she would look at me. I remember making little faces at her as she laughed and smiled. I loved this! How nice it was to have this positive response in someone. But I also worried. I thought that she would grow up and see that I was bad and ugly and evil, then she would no longer smile at me – but that never happened.

As well as pushing the pram, I was involved with basic chores connected with the baby such as washing nappies and sometimes feeding her. I didn't see much of her, however, because I was in my room so much. When Helen left, and I had to take full-time care of Karen, it wasn't easy – I was 11 years old – but I was more than happy to do it.

I remember that first morning after Helen left so well. We were all milling around the house in a state of confusion, yet I was so happy. I just couldn't believe that she had finally gone. The most surprising thing for me was that she had left Karen behind. When Helen had left a year previously for a little while, just after Karen's birth, she'd taken the baby with her. I'd really missed the little one. I'd missed her smiling face as I pushed her in the pram.

As time went on, Karen would beam at me whenever she saw me. Being so small, I had to stand on something to lift her out of the cot but I managed it. I also managed to bathe her and feed her and then spend whole days playing with her. She and I went virtually everywhere together. I finally had someone to love properly in this baby and she loved me back. She would sit on my knee and I would read her stories. I would sing her the nursery rhymes I used to sing to myself as I stood alone in the bathroom or bedroom. I would draw her pictures and I would laugh as she tried to draw. I protected her from her eldest brother nipping and tormenting her. I walked her to and from nursery. I took her to the play park and the swimming baths. I got her to eat things she had never tried. I nursed her when she was ill. I would go to the charity shops and buy her clothes and I would dress her up as best I could.

❧

By the time I left home, Karen was at primary school. I was so desperate to get out of the house and away to start my own life that I just couldn't give much thought to what effect my leaving would have on her. I now know that, at that time, she felt she had been 'abandoned' again. I did feel guilty, and when I visited once or twice in the first year after I left, I went back just to check on Karen, as she was the only one I gave any thought to.

She was my little sister. Ironically, as she has no direct blood link to me, she is the only one I class as being real family. She was the only one who showed me true love during my whole childhood.

I tried to keep in touch with her but going back to the house where so many things had happened to me was difficult. At one time during my twenties when I was living with my fiancé and his parents, I would collect Karen and she would come and stay over. I would take her shopping and buy her well-needed clothes. My future mother-in-law, Flora, was a remedial teacher, and she would sit and help Karen with her reading and writing. I would buy her lots of Christmas presents and wrap them up and take them to her.

But then I abandoned her again.

Before I married, I made a conscious decision to leave my past behind. I couldn't deal with the memories of all the things that had gone on in my childhood every time I visited the house and saw Karen. For my own self-preservation, I withdrew again. In my youth and ignorance, I didn't consider the effect this would have on Karen or what her fate would be when my father died, leaving her homeless. I now know that all of these acts devastated this vulnerable young girl, and that she didn't have an easy time when she went to live with her older brother. I wish I'd had the wisdom and knowledge then that I have now, but I was used to thinking about my own survival first.

I am very proud to say, though, that in spite of what could have been devastating for us – what could have been the end of a bond we made all those years ago – Karen understands now that we were both victims of circumstances way beyond our control, and she has accepted me back into her life.

I am so proud of her because she is a beautiful woman who has managed to carve a nice life for herself with her husband, who she's been with since her teens. They have two lovely, intelligent little girls, and the love in their family is inspiring. This, as far as I am concerned, is a real achievement because it wasn't easy for Karen.

After I left home it was just Karen and my Dad in the house. My Dad was not at all a well man at this time, yet in spite of social work contact she was left to look after him in a sheltered housing complex. She has told me about much of this time she spent with my Dad but I shall respect her wish not to go into the past here. I'll say only this: Karen, I loved you from the minute I saw you. You are my little sister. I know I haven't always been there for you, but now that I am able to put the past behind me I know we have so much to look forward to, as do our children as cousins. You are an amazing young woman. I have enormous respect for you and your husband and I love your two beautiful little girls to pieces.

I want you to know one thing: Helen Gourlay Ford may be your biological mother but I can assure you that you are so very, very different from her. If she'd had only one ounce of your kindness and gentleness then our childhood might have told another story. But the past is the past and now I look forward to the future with you in my world.

Karen, I love you.

꒰

Chapter Fifteen

RING, RING, RING

THE YEAR BEFORE HELEN left was, by far, the worst – given what I'd already been through, that says a lot. Helen was constantly cross and miserable and the parties were more frequent and more horrific for me. I can't understand her justification or motive for any of this. I can only guess that behind the increase in parties and the appalling nature of the sexual attacks on me was some sort of reaction to how she perceived her life and home situation.

As always, I have many more questions than answers. Was she preparing to leave my Dad and so making things worse for me as she knew she wouldn't have access to me soon? Was she punishing my Dad by punishing me? If that was the case, did he explicitly know what was going on? I know I'll never get to the bottom of it all.

There were a number of men involved in my abuse. Some of them I saw only once or twice, but there were also a few who repeatedly raped and abused me. I never knew their names, of course, and I barely saw what they looked like. Sometimes my room would be dark as I didn't have lots of natural light coming in, but at other times I just couldn't bear to look at them or even open my eyes at any point. I guess that just made it better for them – some of them must have wanted my fear and terror as much as they wanted what they were doing to me.

What I do remember is the smell of them.

And what they did to me.

What they, as grown men, chose to do to a child.

~

During the summer holidays when I was nine years old, the obscenities against me reached a new high. I spent most of my time in my bedroom that summer anyway, but there were huge differences in the experiences I had there. Sometimes, in the morning, I'd be told by Helen to 'get up and get up dressed'. I knew this meant there was a chance I might get out into the sunshine for a bit that day. I'd push baby Karen in the pram to the local shops and I'd go to the butcher's and the greengrocer's, and usually the baker's, before returning home. Once I got back, there wasn't much variety in what I was ordered to do. Helen would scream, 'Get to bed, you!' I'd do as I was told – I was well trained – and get out of my clothes, keeping my underwear on, before getting into bed.

What I did next would depend on what I could hear outside.

If there was no party going on or preparations under way, Helen would just want me out of her way for the rest of the day. On those days, I could usually sneak a book out from under my mattress and take it over to the closed door where I got the most daylight seeping through beneath the gap. I could manage to read quite a lot while Helen was busy in the living room. Sometimes, I could even draw if I had managed to hide a scrap of paper and a few pencils or crayons from the others. Helen would have gone ballistic if she'd caught me, but she usually preferred to ignore me completely if I was in my room. Nevertheless, I would continually listen and watch for someone coming near my room.

However, if I got back from the shops with Karen to the signs or sounds of a party being prepared, the day would be quite different, and I would long for the alternative of being left alone for hours on end with no food and no company. I'd hear her getting ready. The music would go on. I would get my usual

81

command to get to bed, but on those days I would go there and sit bolt upright with my arms by my sides while things got under way. Some days, things would happen quickly; other times, it would take longer. I could be sitting there like that for minutes or for hours. I had no control over it, but I knew what was coming.

It's difficult to say exactly how many people were at these parties, but I'd guess around six at the most, including Helen. I only ever heard one other female voice at these events, a woman I didn't know. The parties always started around lunchtime, and they began with three rings on the doorbell.

Ring.

Ring.

Ring.

When I heard those three rings I would freeze. I'd wait for the sound of the footsteps and the shadows passing by my door as the bell was answered and people were welcomed in. The music would have been going for pretty much all of the morning anyway, but it would get slightly louder once guests arrived. There would be talking. There would be laughing. There would be the sound of beer cans popping and I could smell the cigarette smoke.

They were there for a good time.

I just sat there waiting in that little prison of a room. My room was long and narrow and my bed faced the door. On party days I sat there rigid. I sat in that bed in my vest and pants with my book under the mattress, and I waited until he came in.

Whoever he might be that day.

It was always the same ritual. I hear two sets of footsteps and see two shadows under my door. The man and Helen. Then my door opens just enough to let someone in, then the door closes. I pull my knees up to my chest, hugging them close to me, and bury my head under the covers, just like I always do, but he always finds me. Whoever he is that day, he always finds me.

In my mind, in my adult mind, I can still hear the music and laughter. I can smell the smoke, and, as I feel I am back there with him approaching me all over again, there is the added smell of man. I'm not sure if I knew what that was back then, but the stink seems so powerful in my memory now.

In my head, I fall back into my childhood and I know that, depending on which man it is, things will happen. Different things for different men.

Man One likes to stroke my hair.

He sits on my bed and talks quietly to me. Does he think that this makes him a nice man? Maybe he thinks I'll like him if he uses the right words and right tone of voice. Then, perhaps, it will be easier for him to justify to himself what he is doing to me. This man tells me that I am so pretty. He tells me that over and over again. I know that he is lying because Helen tells me that I am an ugly little witch. Ugly. Pretty. I don't think it matters because I'll still hurt. So, this man lies to me some more, but even though he is still talking quietly, like nice men do, I can tell that he is getting annoyed. He wants things to hurry up so he pulls the covers off me. This man pokes at me and prods at me over and over again. He still says that I am a pretty little thing, but his voice is more hurried now and he is getting out of breath. He is touching himself and, although it is disgusting, I would rather that *he* touched his thing than make me do it.

He's talking all the time, saying the same words over and over again as his breath gets faster.

'Isn't that nice?' he says.

'Isn't that nice?'

No. No, it's not. He is still stroking my hair as much as he can with his free hand, but he is pushing my head. He is forcing it down to his thing, making me take it in my mouth while he shakes it until he's reached satisfaction. Then he stops. Smiles at me. 'Wasn't that nice?' he says as he moves towards the door. Like all the others, he taps gently on the inside of my bedroom door and it is opened immediately for his exit. Someone has been waiting outside all of the time he has done those things to me.

Was it Helen? I can hear a woman's voice and a woman's laughter. Has she been waiting there, listening?

Man Two doesn't like to talk at all. He comes into my room as I wait with my eyes closed on the bed and says nothing. He makes some noise, some low noise, while he gets on the bed beside me before pushing me down. He is a big man – everyone is big to me as I'm so little anyway – and he lies on top of me. This man tries to force his thing between my legs. He pushes and pushes and all of the time I'm nearly suffocating. He finally seems to manage. He gets what he wants, and all he does is grunt all the time. It hurts so much. All I want is for it to stop and for me to go to the loo. This man just leaves without even looking at me when he has finished. He taps on the door and exits. I'm left there, wondering if there will be more of them today. I can never relax, even when one of them has gone, because there can always be others. If I knew that there would be no-one else for the rest of the day, maybe I could read a little, but I never know when the door is going to open and Helen will let someone else in.

On some days, Man Three is in my room. He is a combination of Man One and Man Two. Sometimes he will talk to me, some-times he won't – I don't think it makes any difference because they all do what they want anyway. Sometimes he pushes himself into me; sometimes he wants me to touch him; sometimes he touches himself while he says things. There are lots of these men – they blur into each other – but I recognise that some of them have particular things they want to do. To enjoy it more, I suppose. They have particular things they want to do that makes abusing a child better for them. Nicer.

Every time and with every man, I was terrified before and during the acts. Afterwards, I was just sad and sore. I felt dirty and horrible. I always welcomed them finishing their deed and then gently tapping on the inside of my bedroom door to be let out. When they left, I would curl up in a ball and cry and cry, wondering what I had done that was so bad.

❧

Chapter Sixteen

Unanswered Questions, Unwanted Memories

WHAT KIND OF MAN SEEKS sexual gratification from a child? Who are these people? I can guess that they are in some way inadequate; I can guess that they may claim they were abused as children – although, for me, that is one of the most shameful excuses to hide behind. I know that these men are 'normal'-looking men who often have families of their own.

There are many reasons and opinions about what makes a person a paedophile, but I want no excuses or justification. I know their methods and the damage they do. I feel that the most shocking part of my story is the fact that I was made available for these men – in my own bedroom, the place that should have been my haven – by the person who was supposed to take care of me and protect me.

On a few occasions at Helen's parties, I was made to stand in the bathroom and be belted over the bath while people watched my abuse, as if they were at a show. Did Helen sell tickets? I sometimes wondered. Did she profit from my horrors? I do wonder what she got out of it – was it all emotional and psychological? Perhaps she just hated me so much that she wanted me to suffer in every way imaginable, or perhaps she benefited financially. Did men pay her for the privilege of raping me?

༄

Sometimes I get a flashback of a moment, like a movie-clip in my mind. I know it is a memory of something that happened but it is almost as if I am removed from my own body, looking down or in on the situation. I know I don't want to look at this clip because it is too horrible, but, at the same time, I have no control over which memories come in and invade my thoughts.

One such flashback that has recurred over the years is a time in the bathroom of the house in Edina Place. I would have been around nine years old. I don't know what day or month it was, but I remember that it was cold and dull outside, and the rain was tapping on the window. There was no sun this day to warm the room slightly or cast the shadows that I liked. With the sun, there always came spots of light dancing across the room, and there would be an area beside the bath where I could stand and catch a bit of warmth on my shoulder. But there was no sun this day.

I stood with my hands by my sides as I had been told, in my underwear, and with nothing on my feet. I shifted one foot on top of the other, trying to warm one at a time, and I picked a scab on my leg to keep myself amused. I had a feeling that this was going to be a bad day because I had been sent in there first thing in the morning. My older half-sister had taken the other children out, maybe to the cinema if Helen had grudgingly given her the money. That's what was so worrying. If she'd made an investment to get rid of them, she'd want payback. From me.

Helen was really angry with me that day. She'd told me she'd be in to deal with me later. She was always threatening to 'deal with me', or give me the 'something' that was coming to me. I could hear her moving about, coming out of the living room now and again, walking in the hall or going into one of the other rooms. Every time I heard her footsteps and the noise of a door handle, my heart started racing and I shook with fear of her coming in.

Of course she did eventually open the door.

I cowered at the sight of her shape in the doorframe. Helen dragged me by the hair away from where I was standing and threw me into the lobby with a yell. 'Out, bastard!' she shouted at me before turning back in to use the loo herself. After she was finished, she opened the door and I was just as quickly thrown back in. She went into the living room and I heard her music going on. I was, by now, very worried because I had seen that she was 'dolled up': she had make-up on, her hair had been done, and one of her 'good' outfits had made an appearance. I knew all of that meant she was expecting company.

My stomach rumbled with hunger and the fear of what was to come as I went back to standing in position. It wasn't long before the doorbell rang three times. I heard Helen go down the lobby and open, first, the vestibule door, then the big front door to greet her guests. I heard all the voices saying hello to each other and doors closing, then I listened for the footsteps as they got closer. Closer and closer. I made out the shapes of four people through the frosted glass of the bathroom door as they all came into the lobby. One by one, they went into the living room and closed the door behind them. I heard the music – 'Knock three times on the ceiling if you want me' – and the sound of the partygoers opening cans of beer, talking all the while.

I took the opportunity to do two things at this point. The flurry of activity that accompanied the arrival of Helen's friends provided enough of a distraction for me to go for a pee and gulp down a mouthful of water from the tap at the sink by the door. I then sat on the edge of the bath for a few minutes to rest my legs, rubbing my thighs to try and warm them, as I strained my ears to make out the conversation coming from the living room. Most of it was indecipherable but, now and again, I made out the sound of the 'pet name' Helen used for me all the time – 'bastard'. I knew she would be bemoaning the fact that she had to be responsible for me, because I had heard it all before through the adjoining window between my bedroom and the living room. I heard them talking and laughing and I waited.

I can only try now, as an adult, to make sense of what kind of conversation they had in there that prompted the next act.

I heard the living room handle turn noisily. The voices got louder. I watched, shaking with abject fear, as the shapes approached the bathroom. The time had come for my punishment. I just wasn't sure what it was to be this time.

It happened very quickly, and I'm unsure what sparked it off. All of a sudden, Helen was there, standing in the doorway. Right behind her was a woman and two men. I recognised one of the men, but I'd never seen the other before, the one who wore glasses.

Helen stood there, looking down at me with hatred in her eyes. She had one hand on her left hip and the other was holding the tawse. The woman stood directly behind her, looking over her right shoulder at me. Immediately behind her were the two men. Every part of me was shaking as I looked at my stepmother, and tears started burning at the back of my eyes. I forced them back. I knew I couldn't let her see me cry.

'So, bastard,' she said to me, 'what have you got to say for yourself?'

I looked at her and really had no idea what she wanted me to say. All I could do was blurt out, 'I'm sorry, I'm sorry!'

'I'm sorry?' she yelled back at me, then turned to look at her friends. 'Did you hear that?' she said to them. 'She's sorry! What are you?' she said, wanting to hear it again.

'I'm sorry,' I repeated.

Reaching out, she grabbed me by the right arm and, pulling it, she shouted in my face, 'And why is the little bastard sorry?'

'I'm sorry that I've been bad,' I said, because I knew that's what she expected and wanted to hear. At this, she forced me over the bath, pushing me down on the cold metal.

'And what do you deserve when you've been bad?' she yelled at me.

'I deserve to be punished,' I choked, repeating the ritual of fake words that I was now used to. I was so scared and incredibly humiliated because this time I had an audience, an audience who clearly were there for the sport of it rather than to help me. I could hear them moving about but I couldn't see them, although I could feel their eyes on me. I was leaning over the bath, afraid to move, as I waited for that first stinging blow. It came soon enough, as did all the others raining down on my back, legs and backside. I yelped and squirmed and repeated her mantra: 'I am bad, I deserve to be punished.' It was agonising and seemed to go on for ever.

When it did stop, she started yelling at me again: 'Bed, bastard!' I wasted no time in running past the group at the doorway, who had parted to allow me through. I ran as fast as I could into my room, into my bed, where I wrapped the woollen blanket around me like a shield. I cried and nursed myself to sleep. I don't remember much more about that day – what happened, whether her friends stayed on, or what time the others came home. I simply did what I often did at times like this and shut myself out from the rest of the world.

~

Throughout the school summer holidays, I didn't have what other children experienced. So many of them – although not all, I realise that – had little more than boredom to contend with as they spent one lazy day after another. Not for me was there a normal summer day of playing in the street with friends, or a day trip to the seaside. I was there only to be used. Parties would eventually finish (always before teatime). People would leave as quickly as they had arrived and things went back to 'normal'. I would hear Helen feed her own children and laugh with them as she got them ready for bed. Sometimes, after one of these events, I would be allowed up and given tea standing at the table, then I'd do the dishes. Very occasionally, I would be allowed a bath; even more rarely, I'd be allowed to sit on the floor in the living room and watch some television.

My Dad had been working lots of hours at the GPO as well as doing window cleaning. He had been doing this window cleaning for some time before he had an accident; exactly how long I am not sure, but he'd started up what he hoped would be his own business because the Post Office had cut back on overtime. He was still working as a postman but he wanted out of there eventually, and setting up this business seemed to be a good way of earning money and moving on. He was out of the house even more during this time, as he'd leave early to go and do his deliveries, and when he returned in the afternoon he would get changed and go straight back out to wash the windows in our area.

One day, he fell. He had been cleaning a tenement window and was standing on the window ledge outside when he some-how lost his grip and fell 14 feet. He landed on his feet but smashed both of his ankles. He was in hospital for what seemed like months, and while he was laid up, Helen partied.

The day he had the accident I came home from school to find Auntie Madge – my Dad's sister – there instead of Helen. The atmosphere in the house was strange. I could tell this wasn't one of Auntie Madge's usual visits where we would all be on our best behaviour and I would be allowed to stay up. She would usually bring us a comic and a sweetie on these visits, but today there was a look on her face. Finally, she told me the news about Dad's accident. I was so upset. I felt my whole world was going to fall apart. I just kept saying over and over again, 'Is he going to die? Is he going to die?' Auntie Madge said that he wouldn't and that he would be fine, although she warned us that he might not be able to walk for a while, and when he finally did, he'd have crutches.

All I could think about was how awful it was when he wasn't

in the house. I had visions of him never coming home, and I was truly scared about what would happen to me if there was only Helen in my life. Although he was far from the best of dads, life with him was much better than with Helen. For the rest of that day and the next, Auntie Madge stayed over while Helen went to visit my Dad in the hospital. After a few days it was clear that he was going to be in hospital for a while. It was a terrible time. I knew I couldn't ask about him as that would just annoy Helen. I didn't know how bad he was because I was never really told, and there was no way that I was ever going to get to visit him in the hospital.

Meanwhile, to all the people that mattered, Helen behaved as if it was a terrible hardship. When the social worker came, she was so dramatic, saying how terrible it was that her poor husband had had such an awful accident, and how was she going to look after us all now? She said pretty much the same things to Auntie Madge, but when there was no-one like that around, she'd get herself all done up and people would come to the house.

I can still smell the hairspray and cheap perfume she wore. Helen liked to look after herself; she liked new clothes and she loved getting 'dolled up'. She tried her best, I suppose, but I could never look at my stepmother and see anything pretty about her. She wore glasses – the kind that look best on Dame Edna – and she'd had her teeth removed due to gingivitis. As a result, the false teeth clicked in her mouth constantly. Her nylon clothes bristled with static as she walked. Even her birthday was appropriate – 31 October, Hallowe'en! I used to believe that she was a witch because she always made such a big fuss about this day.

I'm sure that Helen must have thought she looked great when she made an effort, but to me she looked terrible because her getting dressed could only mean one thing – a party. At the time of my Dad's hospitalisation, these parties were more frequent – nearly every day – and they lasted longer because my Dad wasn't going to be home from work.

The week before my Dad came out of hospital was the worst

I can remember. The parties were constant, as was the associated horror. On one day, three men came to my room, one after the other, each taking turns to abuse me. Looking back, it seems as if the attacks on me heightened in intensity and number at this time. Perhaps this was because Helen had been told by the hospital doctors just how bad Dad's injuries were, and she was facing the realisation that the parties would have to stop.

When he returned from hospital, my Dad was hobbling pretty badly on crutches. He clearly couldn't work because of the type of injuries he had. In fact, he would have difficulty walking from then on and never worked again. This changed things. From that point on, the parties and the sexual abuse stopped. I'm sure that was purely for practical reasons. My Dad was there so Helen couldn't carry on in the way she had been doing. So, for once in my life, my Dad did protect me, even if it was unwittingly. From the moment he came home, simply by being there, I was safer. The school holidays finished soon after he was discharged from hospital, and it was back to school.

Helen did go out on her own, all dolled up in heavy make-up and Lurex, always at night, always without my Dad. I assume that there were parties elsewhere, but I don't have any evidence. On a few occasions after she'd slammed the door behind her and announced she'd be back 'late', I remember having such a nice time with my Dad. He'd buy fizzy cream soda and a bar of Wall's vanilla ice cream to make ice cream floats. We'd sit together in the living room and watch telly while slurping at the treats. It was all simple enough, but it was what I had dreamed of. These were rare events, but all the more memorable for that.

The contrast of having my Dad at home was immediate, and the dynamics began to change in the house. There were new patterns, though, and every evening would be the same. No sooner would I be in bed than the arguments between them would start. The fighting would go on and on until one night, when Helen Ford finally left my life.

I remember it so clearly.

Around New Year, my Dad and Helen were arguing in the living room. As I sat in my bedroom, cuddling my knees and hearing the hatred between them, I realised that this fight was heated, even by their standards. The voices kept getting louder and the swearing was getting stronger. Suddenly, I heard a loud clattering noise before everything went silent for a few moments. When the shouting started up again, it was largely Helen's voice that I could hear. The words were muffled, but the pitch and tone made it clear that she despised my Dad in every way.

The fact that one of them might leave was, of course, in my mind. Indeed, I'd fantasised about my stepmother going for years; but it suddenly hit me that it might be my Dad who would go. Helen was more comfortable in this house as it had always been her little kingdom. She had her kids to look after, and she was surrounded by friends. If my Dad did go, I'd be thrown back into the pit of horror with parties and men and terror day after day. I could barely breathe as I waited to see (or hear) what would happen next.

The shouting from Helen was interspersed with periods of quietness. I didn't hear my Dad say or do anything at all. I was so used to all of the noises of that house and all the clues I used to get when I would hear footsteps go one way or the other that I knew when she was coming my way. She passed my bedroom door as I sat there, crouched and frozen.

I heard the front door onto the street open.

I heard footsteps walking away outside.

I didn't hear them come back.

I didn't hear them come back!

She had gone.

Helen had gone.

꒰

Chapter Seventeen

THE WOMAN OF
THE HOUSE

THERE ARE TWO STORIES I have about Helen's departure. Her version, which I heard from other people, is that my Dad hit her, and the other is that she hit my Dad.

My Dad and Helen had a friend who used to come round to the house. We called her Auntie Mae but she wasn't a relative; like a lot of children in those days, we were expected to call friends of our parents Auntie or Uncle. She was the only woman I can remember visiting us, apart from Nellie and Madge. Auntie Mae would often come with her daughter, who was younger than me.

Once, when I was around nine years old, I was thrown out of the house by Helen for allegedly stealing a shilling from her purse. I wandered the streets in the cold for what seemed like hours, having been told not to come back. When it got dark, I was very scared – but even more scared of going home.

I was passing the window of Mae's house when she spotted me. She had a main door flat that opened onto the street, and when she opened the door and called to me, I burst into tears. She took me in and made me tea and toast and asked me what was wrong. I told her I'd been thrown out after being accused of taking the shilling. Mae noticed my bruises. She recognised them as having been given in anger; as a victim of domestic violence

94

she was no stranger to bruises herself. She sat me down and asked me to tell her what had happened.

I told Mae about Helen and the beatings. I told her how I felt Helen hated me. Auntie Mae sat and listened to me as I told her about not being fed, and about how scared I was. The only thing I didn't tell her about was the sexual abuse. I was just too ashamed. Mae was a drinker. In fact, she was often drunk when I saw her, but she was a cheerful drunk. In spite of the bruises she often wore on her face, she was a beautiful woman. She was downtrodden and life was hard for her, but she was a good person. As she sat there and listened to me, she held my hand and wiped the tears from her eyes and mine. 'I'll have a word with Helen,' she said to me softly, as she held me. I was hysterical. 'Please, no! No, don't do that, Auntie Mae!' I begged. I was so scared of what my stepmother would do. I was convinced that she would kill me if she knew that I was even at someone's house, never mind that I'd told them about her. I was terrified, but Mae managed to calm me down. She said that it would be fine and that she would make sure Helen didn't touch me.

Auntie Mae put on her coat and, taking me by the hand, led me home. I stood behind her, shaking, as she rang the doorbell. One of the boys answered and shouted to Helen that Auntie Mae was there with me.

I was still shaking and couldn't see how this could possibly end well. Auntie Mae pushed the door aside and went marching up the lobby towards the living room. As she stomped, she shouted back to me, 'Get to your bed, hen, you'll be fine – I promise.' I still didn't dare trust her – I never dared trust anyone – but I sneaked into my bedroom and got into bed as fast as I could. I heard them talking, though I don't know what was said, and I heard footsteps going past my door as Auntie Mae was shown out. I waited and waited for Helen to come into my room but she never did, and she never mentioned the matter to me. I don't know what was said between those two women that evening but whatever Mae did say saved my bacon for the next few days – for that, I'm eternally grateful.

ॐ

After Helen left my Dad, Auntie Mae came round to the house once or twice to check on us. On one of these occasions, she asked me what had happened between Helen and my Dad. I said that I wasn't sure, but that they had been rowing and then Helen just left. My Dad had told me that Helen had picked up one of his crutches and hit him with it, and I told Auntie Mae about this. She replied that was funny because Helen had said my Dad had hit her with the crutch.

Whatever the real reason was, Helen just left.

She left behind her belongings . . . and she left behind her three children.

Everything went quiet that night. It was late December, round about the time of New Year as 1969 faded into 1970. The next morning, the whole impact of what happened sank in. From now on there was to be no more Helen. No more being locked up. No more starvation. No more silence. No more restrictions and hours upon hours being spent on punishments.

No more abuse. Or so I thought.

I would be able to eat. I would be able to talk. I would be able to go outside – I would be free! I just knew she wouldn't be back this time because my Dad was so angry with her. In fact, I had never heard or seen him so furious. Thinking back, and putting two and two together, this may have been the time he found out who Karen's father was. In later years, he told us that up until that point we all thought he was Karen's Dad too. He had known before Karen was born that he wasn't the father – he'd been told by doctors that he couldn't have any more children after he'd had an operation on his prostate gland.

No-one seemed to share my sheer joy in Helen's departure

apart from my older half-brother. My Dad was very sad but also angry. Helen's two boys were tearful, and baby Karen just needed attention.

On the day that followed Helen's departure, my Dad shouted through to me as I lay in bed. In my mind, I had been going through the things I would now be allowed to do, dreaming of a normal childhood and a happy life. When I heard his voice, I dragged myself out of my thoughts and rushed through to the living room. It was such a normal thing for a father to call through to his child, and yet, for me, it was alien to think that he would be doing anything other than chastising me for something Helen claimed I had done.

'Donna?' he said as I walked into the room. 'Sit down, lass. We need to talk.' I don't think I'd ever been asked to sit down in that room before, never mind be offered a two-way conversation. On top of that, I was alone with my Dad – something that had rarely happened on a positive level for years. I remember that he sighed a lot and seemed to be finding it difficult to work out what he wanted to say. Eventually, the words came out. 'Donna, you're the woman of the house now,' he said simply. I was 11 years old! I asked him whether Helen was really gone, and whether she had taken her children with her. He said that, even though she wouldn't be back, all the kids were still there, even the boys whom she had seemed to dote on.

'You'll have to take care of the bairns, Donna,' continued my Dad. 'Helen won't be back, I can promise you that, but you'll need to take her place. Cooking, cleaning – you understand, hen? That's your job now.'

'Just me, Dad?' I asked.

'Aye – the boys can help you when they can manage, but you've got responsibilities now,' he told me. Frances had long gone, but Simon and Gordon were old enough to help. Even Andrew, although younger, was bigger than me in size. None of that seemed to matter. I was the girl, so it was my responsibility. 'Things will be tight, Donna,' continued my Dad. 'I'll no' work again, and everyone will muck in when they're able, but you . . . this is up to you now.'

I was so relieved that Helen had gone – and that my Dad had reassured me she wouldn't be coming back – that I didn't really dwell on the unfairness of it all. A starved, beaten, abused, neglected 11-year-old being in charge of a whole household was still preferable to her returning.

Or so I thought.

'Everything will be fine, Dad,' I said, over and over again. 'Everything will be fine. You won't let her back, will you?' He gave a little snort and said, 'No, no, I won't – you can rest assured of that. And, Donna?' he asked. 'The bairn? Karen's yours now.' She had left the baby! I shouldn't have been surprised really – my own mother had proved just how easy it was to leave babies. 'You'll have to be her Mummy – best start now, best go see what she wants.' I walked through to Karen's cot where she was standing, gurgling and smiling at me as soon as she saw my face. Her nappy was soaked and stinking; Helen obviously hadn't changed her before she left, and my Dad hadn't given it any thought either. I picked her out of her cot – it was a strain on my skinny little arms – and started telling her that I was her Mum from this point on.

༈

Initially, it was hard work. I was a tiny little girl, very weak from being starved. Now I had the workload of a grown woman. I cooked the food that I'd learned about in home economics at school: soup, cheese scones, apple crumble and suchlike. I was given a book by my Dad called *Home Management* from my Auntie Nellie's collection, and I learned from this how to cook other things too – smoked haddock in milk being my Dad's favourite. I was always trying to make him proud of me – doing his perfect meal, running the house, dealing with Karen – but he never really said much, nothing about being proud of me or that I was doing well.

After being denied food for so long, I began to eat anything I could get my hands on, almost as if I was storing it all up in case things went bad again. This made me incredibly ill – in fact, at one point I needed an emergency appendectomy as my body couldn't take what I was doing to it. I'd had the most awful stomach pains, so my Dad took me to the Royal Hospital for Sick Children in Edinburgh. I didn't see him for two weeks until he collected me. He told me it had been impossible for him to make any hospital visits due to the problems he was having with his feet, and also because he had to look after the other children. I do remember my Dad's sister, Auntie Madge, visiting, and I also remember having a lovely time in hospital because I got to do school work, play with toys and have meals cooked for me.

꒱

It was a very strange time for all of us as the dynamics of the house had changed overnight. Even Helen's boys were not as sure as they had been previously. Gordon and Andrew were used to talking down to me. They were accustomed to me being seen only occasionally, and being treated worse than the dog whenever I was let out. Now they had to face up to a different world. Dad sat us all down the day after Helen left and told us how things were to change. Helen's sons were really upset because their Mum had left. They didn't see her the way I did. She was their Mummy and here was my Dad, who didn't share blood with them, telling us she was gone and definitely wouldn't return. The youngest one was crying and the eldest just kept saying, 'What are we going to do?'

All I could see was that Helen, my tormentor and abuser, had gone.

I liked cooking and I liked looking after the baby. However, I didn't like the housework because I had done so much of it when Helen was around and it brought back bad memories. I also didn't like being left with Helen's older son, Gordon, when my

Dad hobbled over to the pub twice a day. He would torment me, just as he had when Helen was still at home, calling me names like pissy pants, black sheep and bastard, and sometimes nipping me or kicking his football at me. Gordon saw no reason to stop now, even though my Dad would tell him off if he caught him.

Helen may have gone but her son was a constant reminder of her. I know that children are a product of parenting, and Gordon was certainly a child who had learned from his mother. Although I was a couple of years older than him, I was very small for my age and hadn't yet learned to stand up for myself. Gordon missed his Mum and blamed me for her leaving. He would often tell me that I drove her to it by being so bad. A big part of me believed that.

༃

By the time I started high school in the autumn of 1970, we had a home help allocated to us by the Social Work Department. Her name was Nora. Nora would come in three mornings a week and clean the house. That woman really had a job on her hands. The place was always filthy, despite my efforts. Sometimes Karen, who was only a toddler, would potter around after me with a cloth, but the boys and my Dad never lifted a finger to do any housework. No-one washed the bath out. The toilet was disgusting, the floors caked in dirt. The cooker could barely be seen for grime. Ironing was piled up in a basket behind the sofa. The fireplace was always full of ash and dog ends that my Dad would flick into it as he sat in his armchair reading the paper or watching television.

Despite having Nora around, there was still a lot for me to do. It was very hard going because my day was so long and I was still only 12. I'd get up around 6.30 in the morning to get Karen ready. I'd give her and the boys some breakfast and then I'd walk the three miles or so to Karen's nursery where I would drop her off around 8am. Then I'd walk a mile and a half to school. When school was finished, I'd walk back to the nursery to pick up Karen, then head home.

In the early days, my Dad would be at home when I got back from school and he'd give me a pound to go and get something for tea. When he started going to the pub in the afternoon and staying there for most of the day, I would have to go to the pub door and ask for him. I would then go off to Laing's, the butcher on Easter Road, and get rissoles or potted meat. If it was a Friday I'd sometimes go to the fishmonger's and get fishcakes. Once a week I went to the steamie to do the washing. After cooking tea and getting Karen into bed, it would be time to clear up, and that was pretty much my routine for every day. There was no-one there to say, 'How was your day?' or 'Do you have homework?' as I do with my little girl now. It was just work and sleep.

Even little things would take up so much energy – things like Karen's nappies. These had to be scraped, washed, steeped in bleach, rinsed, washed again, hung up to dry, taken in when it rained, put out again for a few minutes of sunshine, brought in, and then it all started again. Every part of me was in physical agony, but it came from hard work, not a belt buckle across my ribs.

The upside was that Helen never tried to come back, as far as I can recall. Maybe she contacted my Dad. I don't know – he certainly never said. I began to believe that I was safe. She *had* gone, and although my days were hard and long, I was more settled than I had ever been with her there.

And there was Karen.

I adored that little bundle of laughs and love and, as I've said before, I got something out of it too. I didn't just discover that I was able to love; I also found out that I was capable of *being* loved. The irony isn't lost on me that it took the child of my tormentor to give me something so precious. Karen's affection for me was unconditional. I was her world. I'd whisper to her, 'I'm your Mummy now, Karen,' even though she never once asked or cried for her birth mother.

❧

Chapter Eighteen

GETTING BY

MONEY WAS ALWAYS AN issue in the house – there wasn't much of it at all. My Dad had a weekly pension from the GPO and a small army pension, but because he owned his house and still had a mortgage on it, he couldn't get any money from the 'social'. There was always a plan afoot in the house to make money, but the stack of bills behind the clock on the mantelshelf got thicker by the day. Most of them were unopened and unpaid, and it wasn't long before we had to pay for our electricity, gas and television by putting a coin into a slot. Our telephone was soon cut off, too, and food was what we could afford, mostly soup. We rarely had meat – only on high days and holidays, as my Dad would say.

My Dad found a few methods of trying to raise a bit of cash. One of the things he did – one of the things he got us all to do – was strip wire. Whoever was in and not doing anything would sit down in the living room and take the plastic covering off copper wire. This was time-consuming and unpleasant work, and by the end of it our hands would be aching and covered in tiny cuts. We would all sit on the floor and take lengths of electric wire covered in plastic. We'd cut the plastic off just enough to allow us leverage to tear it, revealing the bright copper wire within. The copper would then be rolled into balls and put aside ready for me to take down to the scrap merchant in Easter Road down by Hibs Football Club. Here it would be weighed and I'd be given cash for it.

My Dad would also get me to take rags there, and I'd get more money for wool than any other fabric. The rags were generally old clothes and blankets that we could no longer use or wear, but sometimes I would go around the doors of our neighbours pretending I was collecting for a jumble sale for the Brownies or Guides. I'd persuade people to part with their cast-offs, taking anything they 'donated'. Sometimes, I even got something one of us could wear. Helen hadn't taken her sewing machine, and this became valuable for me as I was able to alter cast-offs to fit. I'd learned to sew in school in the same way as I'd learned to cook; we were lucky that domestic science lessons were part of the curriculum back then.

↭

It was a life based on scrimping and getting by – and my Dad's needs came before those of anyone else. He spent a lot of time in pubs – and I spent a lot of time outside them, desperately trying to catch him before he spent every last penny on booze for him and his mates. Sometimes, I'd venture inside and moan and moan at him until he relented and gave me a few bob for essentials. I hated doing it – I hated having to squeeze every last penny out of him – but it was rare for him just to give me cash voluntarily.

My Dad was also smoking a lot. Again, his fag requirements came higher than the family's need for food, clean clothes or other things. He smoked Embassy Regal by this stage – it had been Woodbine or Capstan in the past, but he had moved on to Embassy because they came with a voucher. These vouchers were meant to be saved and then, from a special company brochure, exchanged for things like household goods. That wasn't what my Dad did with them, though. Local shops were always willing to buy these vouchers, so we had a stash of them behind the clock on the mantelshelf, ready to be sold on.

Dad's drinking cost so much money, and it took him away from us as often as he could manage. When I asked him why he went to the pub so much, his reply was always the same – he needed the adult company. Dad started going drinking soon after Helen's departure. At first, it was just an occasional lunchtime pint followed by a flutter at the bookies, but soon it increased to him going in at opening time every day at 11.30am, and leaving when it closed for the afternoon around 2pm. He would say that he only went for the chat and to get out of the house, but he seemed perfectly content to sit there all day, playing dominoes, smoking and supping beer.

Whenever my Dad did come home, or when I finally managed to drag him back there, he would sit in 'his' chair by the fire and do little more than smoke, with either a can of Tennent's lager or a cup of tea by his side. My Dad's cup of tea was a ritual. It was made in an old tin teapot on the stove, with 'real' tea leaves, and would sit there all day. In his right hand would be a cigarette, and on his lap would be the *Sun* newspaper. He sat there with that paper in his lap, open either at the racing page or the crossword. His feet would be soaking in a basin of warm water and there he would sit for the rest of the day. Everything would come to him: cups of tea when he wanted; his dinner; the baby for a sit on his lap; a top-up of hot water in his basin; and us if we wanted to talk to him.

Because of his accident, my Dad wasn't very mobile, although he did manage to get to all of those sessions at the pub, and occasionally to the Hibs Club or bowling club! He was in a great deal of pain from his injuries, and on top of that he suffered from chronic bronchitis from the years of constant smoking. He coughed terribly when he got up in the morning; his breathing was laboured and he was developing a humped back due to his limited lung capacity.

༄

My father continued his daily trips to the pub. As I got older, he increased his hours to those of the local licensing laws, going straight in at opening time, coming home for food when it closed for the afternoon, and then back again as soon as it opened at 5pm until closing time at around 10 or 11pm.

On Fridays or Saturdays, he started to bring people back after hours for more drink. They'd have a sing-song or listen to Billy Connolly on the old record player. Sometimes these would be fun times – if they were just singing and laughing, there was a good atmosphere and lots of hilarity, plus I'd get to stay up late.

But, on other nights, there was a different atmosphere. If someone fancied an argument, or if the drinking had gone too far, there was another feel to the house. I hated it. I had thought that the days of parties, music and drunk men were long gone. Now they were back, I found it hard to accept that it was my father bringing these memories into my life again, and I hated myself for thinking it would ever end.

Not only that, he'd invite them to stay. He said that it helped him out financially and helped them out as they had nowhere to go. It was always men who stayed over, some for weeks at a time and others just for a few nights here and there.

༄

Those first few months after Helen left were confusing. I was still sleeping in the boxroom, but now I kept the door ajar and the light on all the time. I still got very scared – how could I forget all that had happened, all that had been done to me? When things got too bad, I would sneak through to the living room and try to sleep on the sofa. Even if the nightmares were too much for me, or if sleep kept itself out of my grasp, I felt better away from where the worst abuses had happened to me.

I wanted Helen to be gone permanently but I was terrified that she might return at any moment. I was given so many responsibilities but didn't really have the physical or emotional capacity to deal with all of them. This might all have been bearable if my father had been more of a man – more like the man I wanted him to be, needed him to be. Helen had gone and my Dad needed to step into the breach. Instead, I was faced with a shadow of a father – drinking, smoking, barely having enough money to keep us all together. This was not the fairy-tale hero Daddy whom I had prayed would rescue me – and it wouldn't be long before I discovered, to my cost, just how useless he was at keeping me safe.

ॐ

We five children were victims – victims of a relationship between two adults – and we were all suffering to varying degrees. The shocking thing is we were still being visited by social workers on a regular basis. They saw the squalor we were living in; they saw that my Dad couldn't cope physically, financially or emotionally; yet we were all left there. Our home help, Nora, left after a little while because she couldn't cope. We once had our walls painted by a group of students, and we received a charity parcel at Christmas time, which was very welcome given that there was little in the way of extra money at that time of year.

I was 12 and a half when I had my first Christmas without Helen (I couldn't remember the ones in Barnardo's). My Dad came home from the pub one night with a book of Provident cheques. These were prepaid savings certificates, almost like gift tokens, which could be exchanged for goods displaying the Provident sign. 'Take these,' he told me. 'Get yourself to the shops and get a few wee things for the bairns.' I looked at him, waiting to see what he would say about me. He didn't offer anything else. 'Something for Karen?' I asked, as she was always my priority. 'Aye, a dolly maybe,' he answered.

I felt something pull at my heart at those words when I remembered the Christmases I had spent wishing for a Tiny Tears dolly. It was all I wanted, all I thought about. Although Helen had started beating me by that stage, she hadn't begun her worst cruelties. She kept asking me what I wanted from Santa. I should have realised there was something amiss as, in truth, she couldn't have cared less. In my innocence, however, every time she asked, I answered, 'A Tiny Tears baby, please,' and she'd laugh as if it was the most hilarious thing she'd ever heard.

On Christmas morning, I could hardly believe my eyes when I walked into the living room and saw a wrapped present with my name on a little tag. I walked over, mesmerised, as Helen and my Dad watched. I picked it up, hardly daring to believe it might be what I wanted so much, but, as I tore the paper off, I had to accept the wonder of Christmas. It was! It was a Tiny Tears dolly box! By this stage, Helen and my Dad were beside themselves with laughter. I opened the box carefully – Tiny Tears must be so precious and delicate, I thought, because it hardly weighed anything. It took a few moments for the reality to sink in. There was no escaping the fact that my Christmas present was an empty Tiny Tears box. What hurt even more than Helen's nastiness was the fact that my Dad was joining in – he must have known what she had planned, and he must have thought it was a good idea. Now, he casually mentioned getting a baby dolly for Karen as if it was the most natural thing in the world.

I held back the tears that pricked at my eyes and asked, 'Gordon? Andrew? Simon? Shall I get something for all of them, Dad?' He didn't even glance up from his newspaper crossword, 'Aye, something for them all.' I walked away, holding the cheques, but he called out to me, 'Donna?' 'Yes, Dad?' I answered – maybe this would be a good Christmas after all. 'If there's anything else, get yourself a wee thing. Only if all the bairns are sorted though.' I thought I might get a Christmas that year, but it didn't look like it – I was bottom of the list, as always, and my Dad hadn't even seen fit to recognise that I was one of the 'bairns' too.

I had to be Santa.

We had chicken on Christmas Day and we were given selection boxes from our social worker. I will always remember that Christmas because there was no tormenting or abuse, but there was precious little happiness or joy either.

᠄

By the time I went to high school, I was completely disillusioned with the education process. Since I'd started school, teachers had never really noticed anything was wrong with me – apart from when I was caught stealing food – and I saw no reason to believe this would change. From about the age of 13, I began truanting a lot. The only subjects that interested me were art and science. I liked art because even I could see that I had some talent there, and science was enjoyable because of my wonderful teacher, Mr Ritchie.

Sometimes it was absolutely unbearable going into school because of the constant teasing and ridicule, and I was confused by the adolescent changes in my body and feelings. Very rarely was there anything in my day to look forward to. On a typical day I would drop Karen off at nursery school then just go off for the rest of the time she was there, usually up to the art galleries or museum in town where I would wander around and look at everything while keeping warm. Although we got 'free dinners' at school (something Helen had stopped while she was around), I preferred not to be at school to get them, taking a jam sandwich with me for my jaunt instead. I would always leave in plenty of time to go and pick up Karen from nursery.

My Dad never once asked me about school or whether or not I went. The truant officer became a regular visitor to our house, concerning myself. It was purely this intervention that made my father insist that I was to attend school. The very thought of going to school was awful for me. I felt stupid. I know that people thought I was stupid too, because I was different, I was scruffy and unkempt. I knew that I had a decent brain because I had devoured all of Auntie Nellie's books; I had helped Simon learn to read; I could draw and there was a part of me that had the desire to make something of myself. But I didn't fit in. I had no friends at school. No-one wanted to know me. My friend, Elaine, went to a different school.

⌇

The only time I really enjoyed school was in my final year, thanks purely to the two new art teachers, Mr Slater and Mr Dalgleish. They were young, fresh out of college and enthusiastic, but most important of all, they encouraged me. I have met both of them in recent years. Mr Slater came along to an exhibition I held in Edinburgh during the Festival in 2007, and I visited my old school in 2006 and spoke to Mr Dalgleish. Both of them taught my niece, Hannah, who is now a very accomplished artist herself. They looked beyond the exterior of the person I was and saw who I was inside. Small details like these allow us to grow. They were good teachers because they did not discriminate. I still treasure a school magazine that features some illustrations I did back then.

I did well at art and managed to pass my Ordinary Grade, but that was the only qualification I achieved. I know I wasn't stupid because I'd read voraciously ever since my Auntie Nellie left all of her library to my Dad, and I had accessed it through the horror of those years in Edina Place. In fact, I was better read than most people I knew, but I just didn't have the support at home to allow me to achieve. I was going back there from school to cooking and cleaning and caring for a little girl. In some ways, I knew that all of these things were wrong but I wasn't really too bothered because I always had a plan to get out of that house and that street.

I knew there was another world out there and I was determined to find it.

༜

Chapter Nineteen

ONLY AFTER ONE
THING . . .

HOME LIFE IN MY TEENAGE years was better than it had been when Helen was there – but it was still terrible. I was growing up, even though I'd had no childhood to speak of. I had so much responsibility – cooking and cleaning for six people, and looking after the younger children – yet not one of my needs was being met.

When I was about 14, my Dad came through to my room one day. 'We need to have a wee talk, Donna,' he said, pretty much always his opening gambit when we spoke about anything he decided was important. I wondered what other task or responsibility he had thought of to give me this time. 'It's . . . well . . . it's stuff that you need to know,' he stuttered. 'Life . . . things . . .' I looked at him blankly; I had no idea what he was fumbling around trying to say. 'The birds and the bees!' he quickly said. 'The birds and the bees, Donna!' Saying this, he shoved a paper bag with the local chemist logo on it into my hands. I looked into it gingerly – inside were the biggest sanitary towels imaginable. I was embarrassed and so was he. I had started my period before this time but I was too ashamed to tell anyone, so I would use rolled-up toilet paper stuffed in my pants. I wonder now if he knew that I had started?

'You'll need these, Donna, when you become a woman,' he told me, not looking at my face at all. 'You'll know what to do, but there's something else . . .' I wondered what else he could possibly say that could be any more embarrassing. 'Boys. Watch out for them, Donna. They only want one thing.' With that, he almost ran out of my room, no doubt proud of himself for doing his fatherly duty.

That was it. That was all he offered. I couldn't even look him in the eye. He'd had men staying over in this house who had abused me – friends of his – and here he was trying to be a Dad? The fact was that I had been sexually abused again in the years after Helen left. In some ways, these later attacks were more awful for me because, for a long time, I felt I was responsible for much of what went on. I don't in any way feel that now because I know I was a child and that these things were done to me without my permission or encouragement. However, I felt guilty and responsible then, and at some points afterwards, because of the way a lot of it happened.

One of the things that used to confuse me was that these men were often nice to me. They engaged me in conversation and gave me attention – things which my Dad rarely did. They flattered me and listened to me. My Dad was always too tired, too distracted or too drunk to actually notice that I was carrying so much and yet being deprived of even basic interaction. It was always just assumed that I would cook and clean and look after everyone. But these men, these men he brought to our home and trusted, they knew how to be nice – and I'm sure that they saw it as an investment worth their time given what their ultimate aim was.

I'm not exactly sure when the abuse started up again after Helen left, but I know there was a fair bit of time when there was no abuse going on. My days then were all about making sure Karen was all right and that the housework was done. I know that when I was 13 and truanting, I was being sexually abused by a man who was sleeping on the settee. I'm vague about when it first happened and who perpetrated it. What I remember most is that, when it happened, it was almost as if I expected it. It was the same pattern repeating itself. I just used to freeze and let it run its course. I had been there so many times in the past that I felt powerless, that there was nothing else to do. I think I was so conditioned to accept sexual abuse that it was almost as if it was a normal part of my life.

There were some specifics I remember though.

There was Dougie, whom I mentioned in *The Step Child*, and who had the audacity to talk to me at my Dad's funeral as if we were old friends, and there were a couple of others.

One man was a regular in Middleton's pub, and became a frequent visitor to our house after the pub closed for the night. He was a bit older than my Dad and very smarmy. Like many of my Dad's drinking friends, he was nice to me. This man (whom I'll call Peter) was married and lived not too far away from us with his wife and young family. He always had a mouth organ in his jacket pocket and he'd bring it out and give everybody a tune. He looked a bit like Hughie Green and he was keen on singing when he wasn't playing the mouthie, even although he wasn't too good. If I was ever there when Peter sang, he sang to me directly.

It took a long time for him to get what he wanted from me.

I thought he was just being nice, and I so desperately wanted someone to be nice to me and give me attention. Peter did just that. He would bring me little gifts, pay me compliments and sometimes give me a hug just like I thought a Dad would. It all changed one night when he asked me to meet him outside at his van. I did, thinking nothing of it, and then he asked me if I wanted to go for a drive. I jumped at the chance; I always welcomed any opportunity to get away from where I lived.

We went for a drive down to Portobello and then up to Holyrood Park – and at some point we stopped. I can't remember where now, but it was a quiet place. Peter was a great joker and a charmer, and he always kept me talking and laughing. He'd often given us some out-of-date food as he worked for a grocer. He knew we had very little, and the tins he gave were always welcome. On this occasion, he said he had some in the back of the van and asked if I'd tell him what I wanted. 'Take your pick,' he said to me. So, I did. I went into the back of the van to see what charity I could get this time from this nice man who wanted to help out.

I don't know how it all happened, but he started kissing me and kissing me. I was really uncomfortable and scared and kept saying that I needed to get home. I was so unprepared for this change of direction from this man I had begun to trust. I tried to push him off and get away from him but I couldn't.

Before I knew it, I wasn't with a man I could trust any more. It felt as if I was back in my boxroom and it was all happening again. So, I did what I had learned to do, what I had been groomed to do -- I just froze and let it happen.

Peter successfully raped me and, as he did, I wondered what had happened to the sanitary towel I was wearing. I also wondered whether this was just what all men do, and what I had done to deserve this.

Afterwards I was too embarrassed to think about anything except getting away from him. On the way home he tried to talk like he did before but I couldn't hear him; I couldn't hear the words or the lies. When he dropped me off, he complimented me, but it sounded pathetic now. I ran into the house, scrubbed myself in the bath and went to bed where I hugged my knees and cried and cried. My face was stinging from his stubble, I was very sore and I was mortally embarrassed because I had my period. Most of all, I was hurting inside. What was wrong with me that men wanted to do this to me?

Helen was right – I was evil.

Chapter Twenty

୬

MY WORLD

I HAD ONLY TWO FRIENDS IN my teenage years and a bit of a social life via the local youth club. However, I did manage to persuade my Dad to allow me to go on two weekend trips with this youth club – one to Iona and one to Eddleston in Peeblesshire. How I treasure the memories of those times! The youth club gave me a little outlet from my home life, which was almost unbearable.

Karen was the only good thing about life at home. I would read to her, play with her and bathe her. I would take her to the park and the nursery. She needed me and I loved being with her, but I was sad and moody a lot of the time. I was always frightened because I never knew when I would next be asked to do something I didn't want to; I never knew who my Dad would ask to stay over and what they would do to me.

My Dad never noticed anything was wrong with me. He just put my moods down to my age, but the truth was I was angry with him. I was angry with him because he hadn't seen what was happening to me when Helen was there. I was angry because the very people he called friends were abusing me. I was angry because he was always at the pub, and when he wasn't he just sat in his chair feeling sorry for himself.

I was still a child but I would soon be a woman, and I was beginning to see that I could get away from all of this. My only concern was little Karen. My Dad was incapable of looking after himself, let alone being responsible for a little girl, and I was filled with horror thinking that she might end up being abused if I left. Looking back, I can't believe what possessed the Social Work Department to allow this vulnerable little girl to remain in the house. By the time I was 15, she had started primary school and, up until this point, had been my main focus because she needed me so much. I really was her mother from the moment Helen Ford left. Her brothers had been seeing quite a lot of Helen, and Karen had been to see her a few times too, but she was always unhappy when she returned. It was a terrible environment for a little girl in both places but Karen was happier at my Dad's as it was all she knew.

I knew that, as far as I was able, I'd never let any harm come to Karen. I loved her so much, and I think Karen felt that, but I knew that I was going to have to leave at some point. Karen loved my Dad too, and he loved her back. I remember her climbing onto his lap and hugging him. She was such a lovely, happy, cherubic little girl that it would have been hard not to love her. She was the only pure thing in that whole house, in my whole life, and it breaks my heart even now to realise what she had to put up with unnecessarily, because it was Karen who was left to care for Don Ford when everyone else had flown the nest. She wasn't abused in the way I had been but she was neglected. The house was a mess, my Dad was crippled and she was still just a little girl in the middle of it all. For many years I felt wretched and guilty for leaving her. I had mothered this baby and done my best, but I just couldn't live in that environment any longer. I was dying from it all and had to get away.

&

Looking back on my childhood, you might think there would be absolutely nothing I'd want to recall from those days. I have recounted how people like Helen and her friends exploited me; how my father failed in his role to protect me; and even how the people who were supposed to be overseeing the care I was receiving at home, such as the social workers, failed to act on the obvious warning signs of my suffering. But there were also those who had a positive influence on me, such as Auntie Nellie, and because of that I was able to come through a desperate time with at least some sense of right and wrong.

The world in which we lived was a poor one – not just for us, but for many others living in the area. My immediate environment – the houses in Edina Place and Easter Road – are places that hold too many bad memories. But I do have fond recollections of times spent away from the home, of places and sights I saw back then. When I wasn't at home, apart from the times I was sent on errands by Helen, I was free to think and look and enjoy the sights and sounds that many people may take for granted. And I did. I feel proud to be a citizen of Edinburgh because it is a very beautiful city. It has changed dramatically since my childhood days but it remains elegant and familiar, albeit within a more cosmopolitan setting.

The Easter Road of the 1960s was a very different place from how it is now. Most people stuck to their own street. Someone living in Edina Place would rarely venture further than their own front door; and going 'up town' to Princes Street was quite an occasion and warranted wearing Sunday best clothes.

On a Friday afternoon, Easter Road and its environs were reminiscent of a painting by LS Lowry as the printers and crystal works closed shop for the weekend. At the sound of the hooters, people would spill out from the factories clutching their brown paper wage packet, happy for another week of work to be over.

Children would play in the street – hopscotch, British bulldog, Levoy 21 (a catch-and-find game), elastics, skipping – and mothers would chat on doorsteps. Now the streets are filled with cars vying for parking spaces and the shops are wholly unrecognisable. There are now Polish delicatessens and smart coffee shops where there were once family butchers and grocery shops selling mince by the pound or tea by the ounce. The bookbinders on Bothwell Street is now smart flats, and what were the whisky bonds on Commercial Street are home to restaurants.

Sometimes a glimpse of some aspect of Edinburgh – a sight or a sound – can transport me back to when I was very young. Walking up Easter Road one day recently to visit my niece Hannah, I caught a glimpse of Arthur's Seat, jutting up and scraping the sky between the buildings at the top of Easter Road. For one moment, I was returned to a second in time when I was sitting on the street corner outside Miele's, the chip shop at the top of Edina Place. I would often sit there if I was allowed out to play because it was warm and because I could see Arthur's Seat. I would sit and dream that if I could just get to the top of that majestic hill then I could maybe fly away from all my troubles. It would fill me with wonderful warmth. Seeing it again made me smile because I realised I *did* get away. I didn't fly but I did escape.

Edinburgh at Christmas time has this effect on me too. The multicoloured twinkling lights in the city centre in December can easily whisk me back to my very first Christmas at Leith Walk Primary School. It was the only magical Christmas I can recall from my childhood because I'd been back home for only a matter of months and was allowed to enjoy the moment. I even had a party dress – it was so pretty, and there were little slippers, like ballet shoes. The party was held in the school hall where there was a big Christmas tree with brightly coloured baubles and shiny streamers that twirled and spun. We played games such as ring-a-ring o' roses, the grand old Duke of York and dusty bluebells, and Santa Claus visited when we sang 'We Wish You a Merry Christmas'. It was magical and innocent, and for that moment in time I was a happy, normal little girl.

I didn't know at that point that I would never see a Christmas like it again in my own childhood. In the dark years that followed, I clung to that memory to give me solace. As an adult I'm ridiculous when it comes to Christmas. Santa still comes down our chimney and fills up stockings, and my tree is always reminiscent of the one in my memory all those years ago, gaudily decorated with bright baubles and twinkling lights. Rather than look back at what I didn't have, I choose to remember the times when I did have something, and Edinburgh plays a big part in that memory for me.

❧

Chapter Twenty-one

WORDS OF WISDOM

WHEN I WAS 15 AND GETTING ready to leave high school, one of the few social events in my life so far took place: the Leavers' Dance. Dad gave me a Provident cheque to go and get an outfit for this occasion, only because I'd pestered him so much, saying that I really wanted to go. I don't know why it was so important to me because I can't even remember who I went with, or indeed if I actually went with anyone.

There was a little clothes shop next to our old house on Easter Road – a boutique, as it was called then – and they took Provident cheques. I bought myself a new dress for the first time. It was green and fitted like a glove. I also bought a pair of black wedge shoes and new tights. I wore kohl around my eyes and mascara. My most distinctive memory is not of the dance, nor who was there or indeed whether I was asked to dance by anyone. It was of me standing on a dining chair looking at myself in the mirror in, for the very first time, a brand-new outfit I had chosen.

As I brushed my hair, my Dad paused beside me. There was no contact, no warmth, just a few hurried words: 'Watch yourself tonight,' he said. 'Watch those boys that'll be there – they're only after one thing. Don't give it away.'

I was incredulous.

I'd been getting raped under this man's roof since I was at primary school and now he was offering words of advice about the ways of men.

There weren't many times when my Dad offered me advice while I was growing up. Going by that example, it may have been just as well. In my teenage years, I didn't really want to listen to anything he had to say because I didn't respect him. I sometimes thought I was just being horrible because I was ashamed of him. He was nothing more than a little, broken man sitting in an armchair with a fag and beer can or cup of tea. When he wasn't doing that, he was in the pub with his cronies. To hear him offer me advice was abhorrent. As his words came out, I'd be thinking, 'Too late, Dad, far too late. I'm soiled and I'm damaged and it's all your fault.'

I was still worried about leaving Karen, but I knew that I had to get out of that place or I'd be stuck there for ever. It was about survival. As soon as I sat my one O Grade, I left school. I took a job at Andrew White's, the bookbinders on Bothwell Street, where I had the task of counting reams of paper. I really wanted to do the paper marbling but I was told that it would take me years to work up to that level. Before long I had a very sore back from carrying around heavy reams of paper and standing for hours on end. It would have been hard anyway but I found it really testing because of the number of beatings I'd had as a child.

I hated the tedium and drudgery of this 8am to 4.30pm job, with its 10-minute tea break in the morning, and 45-minute lunch break where you would eat a cheese sandwich and drink a mug of tea while gossiping about the people on the other floor. The only highlight of the week was on a Friday when the hooter would sound a little earlier than every other day, and people would stream out of the building and queue up for their pay packet.

It did, however, bring in £12.50 a week. I was allowed to keep five pounds from this wage and the rest went to my Dad for board and lodgings. I remember buying school clothes for Karen with one of my first-ever wages because I wanted her to look nice.

~

As I got older, I learned how to avoid the men who came back to my Dad's. Indeed, they more or less stopped coming around when they realised that I would just make myself scarce or be busy, or always have Karen or one of the others with me. I still hated living there though. I didn't want to work in a factory for ever, and I didn't want to sit around and watch my father drink and smoke himself to death while my life disappeared too. My Dad wanted me to continue working at the printers because it was a 'good steady job', but I needed to get out. I had lots of arguments with him around this time because by now I realised I just didn't respect him. And he thought I was being irresponsible when I eventually gave up the job I had always hated.

I went to see a careers officer and told him I wanted to be an artist. The man I spoke to said that it was a field far too difficult for me to get into because I had no qualifications. When I told my Dad I wanted to be an artist, his one comment was that I didn't stand a chance because I couldn't draw horses! Guess what, Dad? I can draw them now.

I managed to find a job with the grand title of 'finishing artist' with a company called Ian Fraser Designs, situated in the St Leonards area of Edinburgh. This company produced blown plastic relief pictures of scenes such as gypsy caravans, tramps and animals with a 'flock' background. The base coat was spray-painted onto the picture then it was my job to paint in the details. I stayed there a couple of months then decided it was time that I left Edinburgh. I didn't think about it. I just left.

When I moved out of my Dad's house, I just wanted to get as far away from everything as I possibly could. I had no idea where to go really, but I knew I wanted to get right out of the capital. I went up to Waverley railway station with the bit of money I had and a carrier bag full of my meagre belongings. Choosing Inverness as my destination, I bought a single ticket. No return. I remember choosing Inverness because I knew someone who had come from there, and when he spoke of it, it sounded like a lovely place.

When I was on the train, I got chatting to a couple who had a little baby with them. They asked me where I was going, and I told them I was heading to Inverness to find some work. They were really friendly and, as we chatted more, they discovered I had nowhere to stay at my destination. By the time the journey came to an end, they had offered me a room in their house in return for looking after the baby while they were working, as well as being responsible for cleaning the house for them. I shudder to think now how innocent and trusting I was. I took up their offer because I had nowhere else to go and, as we travelled, it was getting dark.

I telephoned home to let them know I was okay and where I was, but really, all I wanted to know was how Karen was. She was my only concern, but even she at that point couldn't keep me in that environment a moment longer.

Inevitably, the arrangement with the couple from the train didn't work out. I was basically to skivvy for them 24/7, and I felt no better off than I did at home. Even the room they gave me was no more than a cupboard without a window. I knew I had to get out of there. My opportunity came when I saw an advert in the local newspaper for auxiliary nurses with 'live-in accommodation'. I phoned up one day when the couple were out working and, taking the baby with me on the bus, I went for an interview. To this day I don't know how I managed to get the job. Maybe the interviewer took pity on me, or perhaps they really believed my over-enthusiastic warblings about how I wanted to be a nurse (which wasn't true as I still dreamed of being an artist). I told them I could start immediately, and I did – the next day. I can remember going back to the home of the people I was working for with their baby and feeling such an amazing sense of achievement. I had got a job and with it came my very own bedroom with clean sheets, towels and a window!

I was given a uniform – a yellow nurse's dress with white shoes and a little white hat. The work in general was very easy: making beds, changing water jugs, moving patients around, bathing them and suchlike. I found it very straightforward and, in return, was paid a wage and had somewhere nice to stay.

In Inverness, I felt a million miles away from Easter Road – and my Dad and the men – but I missed Karen and still felt really guilty about leaving her. My monthly wage seemed like a fortune. I could have spent it all on myself, buying new clothes and nice things, but I sent two-thirds home. This helped to relieve my guilt a bit, but it didn't take away the nightmares.

Although I was physically away from the horrors, they were still very much with me emotionally. I thought I could just bury my past and flee to a new life, but in reality I was very ill-equipped. I had no social skills, and the experiences I'd had with men had badly scarred me. I was at a very big disadvantage out there now in the world on my own.

৵

I worked at the hospital for almost a year and made some friends. I bought a second-hand bike and would cycle for hours around the streets, right out to Loch Ness and around the loch itself. I bought my clothes in the big Oxfam shop down by the river. It was like a warehouse where all the clothes were set out as if for a jumble sale. I wore vintage blouses with faded jeans and I grew my hair long.

The hospital I worked in, the Hilton, was a geriatric hospital. Most of the patients had suffered strokes or were unable to look after themselves any longer. I loved spending time with them, listening to the stories of their youths. One old lady, who reminded me of my Auntie Nellie, had spent many years in India as her husband had been a major in the army. She would tell me wonderful stories about her big house in Rajasthan where she had servants. Before I left that job, she gave me a silver compact, which I still have to this day; it has a picture of an Indian palace embossed in black on the lid.

Many of the old people were from the Islands – Stornoway and the like – and spoke Gaelic. I learned words in Gaelic from them and loved that too. After a while, I was given the job of assistant to the occupational therapist. With this post came the chance to do crafts with the residents to keep them occupied. I learned more from them than they did from me; one old lady even taught me how to crochet. I was doing my job really, but, inadvertently, I was making them feel useful by getting them to teach me things rather than the other way around!

Then, just as suddenly as I arrived, I decided to leave. A friend from Edinburgh came to visit me from time to time and, on one occasion, he persuaded me to go back, saying that I could get the same work as I had in Inverness, but in Edinburgh. So I upped and left. At first I shared his student accommodation in Old Dalkeith Road. It was all predictable – he used me for sex but rarely even took me out with him.

Eventually, I managed to get myself a job in the City Hospital, again with geriatrics and, again, with live-in accommodation. In complete contrast, I hated working there because the old people were put in a day room from morning till night with little or no stimulation, and were often drugged up with a mixture called a Brompton cocktail. I don't know what that was but I believe it had morphine in it, among other things. It was horrible. When I got the chance to apply for a job in a children's home I jumped at it. The next chapter in my life was about to begin.

๛

Chapter Twenty-two

LOVE

MY ADULT LIFE, IN MANY ways, began when I returned to Edinburgh following that brief period as a nurse in Inverness. I found myself working in a residential home for youngsters being admitted to care; youngsters who had experienced some of the horrors I recognised all too well from my own childhood. So many terrible things had happened to me as a child, and just one of those things should have warranted me being taken away from the situation I was in and protected.

Sometimes children would come into care and I would genuinely wonder why they were there. I can't be too specific here, but there were certain children who should have remained at home with the people who loved them. One child was looked after by two aunts who absolutely adored him but they had a problem dealing with his diabetes. As far as I was concerned, support should have been offered to them in the home rather than taking that poor child away. Another, more extreme, incident was a situation where three children were taken away from their mother after she stabbed their father. This woman had suffered sustained beatings by him, really horrific stuff, and she had finally blown. She was sentenced to seven years' imprisonment. This mother adored her children and they adored her. I felt very strongly that these children shouldn't have been made to pay for this 'crime' by losing their only surviving parent.

Then there were times when children – some as young as three – would be admitted in the middle of the night, having received terrible injuries at the hands of a parent or carer; injuries I recognised only too well. Many of the members of staff were able to comfort and console these children, hugging them and soothing them. I could play with them and do practical things for them, but I'd not yet learned how to hug them. I knew that I could hug Karen easily, but she was my little sister and that was different.

I realised that the anger I felt watching displays of affection came from the fact that I had a huge problem with close contact. It was almost as if I had to set myself challenges. My first task became clear – I had to learn to cuddle and accept physical closeness.

One of the girls who worked beside me was called Elaine. She was a beautiful tall girl with long curly red hair, reminiscent of a pre-Raphaelite painting. Elaine had a wonderful sense of humour and would always have us laughing at any opportunity. The most important thing of all was that she was one of those girls who thought nothing of hugging people. She would just come up and hug you for no reason! At first I found this difficult and I can recall feeling myself freeze, going absolutely rigid at this innocent display of genuine affection. As time went on, however, I grew more and more responsive to her hugs, and before long I was able not only to receive but to give as well.

Those few initial steps towards recognising how I needed to put myself together coincided with two other important developments in my life. First, I was put in charge of an art group in Canaan Lodge – the children's home – and received the first acceptance of my artistic talents I'd ever experienced. Second, I met my future husband.

Meeting Robert was my first big breakthrough. I adored him from the moment I saw him. First and foremost, I liked the look of him, especially his big brown soft eyes, the same eyes our daughter Claire has. As I got to know him, I liked his gentle ways most of all. He was intelligent and kind, and had no problem sharing his knowledge.

I used to go out with other members of staff at the children's home who were the same age – to the local pub or downtown to a disco. What was important here for me was that I was accepted. I was just like all the other young people. They had come from good homes and been reared with strong values but they didn't see the scars or the filth I felt was etched on me.

Robert played a huge part in my transformation. On one of our evenings out in the pub with all the others he asked me out on a date, a proper date! I was bowled over, excited and nervous, but I needn't have been. Our first date was wonderful. We met in a local pub and had a few drinks before going for a meal. It was so lovely, so normal. Robert walked me back to the children's home and was very gentlemanly throughout, even when he kissed me. He asked if we could go out again, and of course I said 'yes'.

The more we saw of each other, the more we fell in love. He never came on to me; he never asked anything of me and he would say lovely things to me. He told me that I was beautiful and that he adored me. These words were so alien to me, words I had never heard before. It was easy and wonderful and very, very normal. I never told him about my past because I didn't want anything to sully this special time. All that I told him was that we were very poor. Robert never asked any more than that as he just liked me for me.

This was my first real reciprocal adult relationship. It was also my first opportunity to discover that I could enjoy sex, although that took a long time to happen. When we eventually made love for the first time it was the most natural thing in the world because that's what it was – making love. Meeting Robert turned my life around. Just as importantly, he came with precious baggage – a loving family.

His Mum and Dad lived in a big detached house in the grounds of Greenlea Old People's Home where Robert's Dad was the officer in charge. As our relationship developed, I began living with them, although in a separate bedroom. When Bob and Flora heard that it was going to be my 21st birthday they said that they would like to throw a party for me. This was a revelation. As they had a big garden we decided it would be nice if we had a garden party, so that's what we did. There was a barbecue, a buffet and music outside. All my friends from work were there, as well as all of Robert's friends. It was a party that I had never seen the like of before, a proper, happy party with dancing and singing and lots and lots of fun. It was the party of my dreams and, to top it all, we then got engaged and moved into our own home together.

My life was finally beginning.

༜

Chapter Twenty-three

CONTRASTS

THE HAPPIEST MOMENTS OF MY life are etched in my mind so deeply that I can call on them whenever life is hard and I feel at a low point. Those moments are my relationship and marriage to my first husband Robert, the births of my three children, and my achievements as an artist. These memories are magical – the times when I have truly been at my happiest.

I called on this magic throughout relationships that were threatening and abusive; and I called on it again when my world was being turned upside down by researching my past. Doing this reassured me that I had succeeded, and that I was entitled to wonderful experiences. I haven't enjoyed looking into my past because of the pain and distress it has caused me, and because so much of it is ugly and wrong, but it is comforting to know that some areas of my life – the areas I have had control over – have been good and rewarding.

I have been married twice. The two marriages – and weddings – were in stark contrast to each other. When I married Robert, I was young, happy and in love. I looked forward to my life with my husband, to building a home together and planning our future. I thought we would be a couple for ever. Robert proposed to me by getting down on one knee. We each chose a ring, and mine came from a little jeweller called Bassi in Bruntsfield, south Edinburgh. They designed and made all their own pieces, and I was so pleased to have a say in what my ring was to look like. I chose a tiny gold lovers' knot with two perfect diamonds sitting in each of the loops. It was such a pretty ring and I was overjoyed with it because it was the nicest thing I had ever owned. More importantly, it united me with the man I was madly in love with. The ring for Robert came from a jeweller in Edinburgh's Rose Street called Scott's. His was a masculine square band striped with yellow, red and white gold.

Robert had many friends from school and we would all meet as a big group to go to dances and parties or just to each other's houses. Sometimes we went on holiday together. Many of these friends got engaged and married at the same time as us, and we all loved to show off our engagement and wedding rings and talk about our plans.

Our wedding was very different from those of most of these friends. They had grand plans, and most of the girls had mothers who took them to look for dresses, organised invites and dealt with all the machinations that go into a wedding. Robert and I set about trying to organise it ourselves, and I think this was the first time it hit me how different I was from other people.

I didn't have a clue how to organise a wedding so I was fortunate to have a good friend called Maura who had worked with me in the children's home. Maura was a little bit older than me and was to be my maid of honour. She helped me look for a dress and for shoes and all the things that go with a girl's big day.

I have such fond memories of Maura. She was a lovely, kind person and great fun, almost like an older sister to me, given that I felt I no longer had my real one. She left the children's home because she wanted to start a family, but we kept in touch with each other. When she gave birth to twin boys I often travelled down on the bus to Penicuik where she lived to help her out; it was a struggle for her as one of the boys was quite poorly. Her husband was a wine merchant and had a cellar full of the most wonderful bottles. One time when I visited we opened one of these bottles of wine after a hard day of seeing to the twins' needs. When her husband came home from work and spotted the wine bottle almost empty, he said to us, 'Did you enjoy that, girls?' We'd thought it was wonderful, which was lucky given that he told us it was vintage and worth about £50, a fortune back then!

Robert's Dad organised and paid for our service and reception. With his help, we had the best wedding ever. We were married in Queen Street Registry Office on 12 June 1981, just a week after my 22nd birthday. I felt funny that day – happy, but odd. I was delighted that I was going to marry the man I loved, and I was so appreciative of all that his parents were doing, but I was obviously aware of the fact that I had no real family beside me on what should have been the happiest day of my life.

I remember beaming from ear to ear when Robert kissed me as we were declared man and wife. As I looked around at that moment, I saw Robert's Mum and Dad, his two sisters and their husbands, my two-year-old nephew Matthew, my little niece Hannah, who was only a couple of weeks old, and our mutual friends. I felt full of love and belonging for the first time in my life.

From the registry office we were driven to the hotel in Humbie where we had our reception. It was a beautiful Scottish baronial mansion set in its own grounds with wonderful gardens. At the end of the day Robert carried me over the threshold of our house, which was next door to his parents' home. This was the first night we spent in this house together. Up until that point we had lived with Robert's Mum and Dad. Through respect for them, we'd slept in separate bedrooms, even though we were enjoying a healthy and happy sex life by this point. I was in love and I really belonged somewhere.

As we honeymooned in Corfu, we made plans for our future.

How could I fail to be happy in a world so very far removed from the one I'd known as a child? I was loved and protected, but I was also young and, at last, I was allowed to enjoy the wonders of my youth.

⸙

Chapter Twenty-four

Mr and Mrs

I LOVED THOSE EARLY DAYS OF married life, of making a home. I painted and decorated our little cottage and made all my own curtains. I cooked lovely meals for Robert and we went out with our many friends. For the first time I was a homemaker in the real sense of the word as I was making a home for me just as much as I was for Robert.

Our life was a little eccentric, I guess. Robert loved animals and we had a menagerie which included a parrot, some lizards and a golden Labrador called Sally whom we would take for long walks up the Pentland Hills. We travelled a lot, holidaying in Greece during the summer of our first year together and going on weekend trips to Amsterdam or over to St Monance in Fife with Robert's Dad.

The pair of us would often babysit for Robert's older sisters, Fiona and Andrea. I loved my nephew and niece, Matthew and Hannah, from the moment I met them. I painted a wardrobe for each of them – Matthew had a brightly coloured jungle scene all over his. He was fascinated watching me paint, and leaned on my shoulder as I covered the wardrobe with snakes and monkeys, lions and tigers, all hidden in green tropical foliage. Hannah's, in complete contrast, was painted with butterflies and flowers.

They are grown-up now, and we all laugh at the stories I still like to tell them of my nappy-changing exploits. They love to hear of the times when they were little, and I am so happy to be able to give them some of those memories knowing that they were safe and protected as children within a loving family. These were happy, wonderful times and it seemed as if nothing could ever spoil the joy I was feeling.

Robert left his job in the Social Work Department and set up his own business in the grounds of a garden centre, selling both tropical and pond fish. This was the business that was intended to set us up for life. He sold ponds too, and would fit them into people's gardens, full of plants and koi carp. I still worked in the Social Work Department. I had moved from the children's home just before we got married. Word had gone around that they were going to close this big home, and many of the staff were being moved to smaller units throughout Edinburgh. I decided to move before that happened and managed to get a position working in an adolescent unit in the Southhouse area of the city.

This transition was quite strange for me. I was happy to be moving, even though the move brought with it a certain amount of trepidation. I was settled in the place where I'd been working; I had lots of friends there, and was a little worried that I wouldn't find this in my new environment. Luckily for me that wasn't the case, and I soon made friends with the staff in the unit and the young people who were resident there.

The only blot on this new landscape came in a confrontation I had with someone else who worked there. This man was an older member of staff in a relatively senior position. I didn't take to him from the word go because I saw in his character some-thing I didn't like, something I recognised from my childhood. Very soon, I could see that he intimidated many of the young people there. He was a bully and extremely threatening, quite a loathsome man.

The unit was small, with around 12 young people living there.

Usually, there were two members of staff on shift at a time. One evening when I was working there with him, I witnessed at first hand his bullying behaviour towards the young people. I just couldn't stand it. I was outraged – he was misusing his position of authority, and being abusive to the very people he was supposed to be protecting. All my sense of injustice and unfairness about my own childhood flared up at that precise moment, and I challenged him. He obviously saw me as a young person too. I was only 20 at the time and looked very young for my age. He then started bullying me and threw me out of the unit, saying I'd been sacked.

He had no authority to do this, so I went to a phone box and called a very senior member of staff at the Social Work headquarters. It ended with me taking out a grievance procedure against this man for his conduct. He was demoted and put under supervision, but continued to work in the unit. A few years later, he was finally sacked over another incident. This time I wasn't involved. Why he was ever given a job in the first place is beyond me. What I did take from the incident was that my sense of there being bad in people was heightened, no doubt due to my childhood abuse, and that I should be aware of this part of me.

While this business was going on, it was a difficult time for Robert and I because it threw up things for me from my past. I still didn't tell him anything. I just couldn't. I was very stressed during this period, and for a while I was unable to be as intimate with Robert as we had previously been. We did argue a little about it but I refused to even consider that it might have any connection with my childhood. At that point, those years were buried for me – or at least that was what I thought.

We did get over things and our life sailed along as normal. I helped him with his new business when I could and we went back to having fun together. I liked my job but was beginning to look to the future, and took various night classes in art, English and history. I passed all of my exams in these subjects and felt good about myself. I also started to learn to drive. Inspired by the fun we had with our niece and nephew, Robert and I began discussing when we would start a family.

We were looking to the future, but my past was still there, waiting to creep into my life again.

Chapter Twenty-five

OBLIGATIONS

WHEN I WAS IN MY TWENTIES, my father was admitted to hospital. He was suffering from emphysema, as he had done for years, but now he had also had a stroke so things were looking particularly bad. With enormous trepidation I went up to Edinburgh's Royal Infirmary to visit him. I say with trepidation because I hadn't had any contact with him for a couple of years as I had decided to get on with my life with my new husband and put the past behind me.

I was shown into the big ward where he was and pointed in the direction of his bed. Don Ford, my Daddy, lay there in a big hospital bed. He looked like a very weak and broken man, surrounded by hospital paraphernalia and struggling to breathe. Looking up at me through his thick glasses, in a laboured way he said, 'Hiya, hen!' as if it was only yesterday that I had seen him.

On that first visit, we made small talk; he asked me to get him cigarettes and I refused. He had hospital pyjamas on that were far too big for him and, as I stood there uncomfortably, I cringed with embarrassment at the thought that this was my father. I'm ashamed to say that I just wanted to get out of there.

After being on the ward for 10 minutes or so, I was taken aside by one of the nurses who, knowing that I was his daughter, asked me many questions about his lifestyle and suchlike. I answered as best I could; I couldn't really give her any information as I hadn't seen my Dad for such a long time. I was uncomfortable, but I couldn't leave just yet as the nurse wanted to explain a few things to me. She said that he was malnourished, and that they were having difficulty getting him to eat. She paused and then asked if I could maybe coax him to have a few mouthfuls of something. I reluctantly said I would try. So the nurse went off and returned quite quickly with a bowl of scrambled egg. Handing it to me, she said: 'If he doesn't eat, he'll die.' To be perfectly honest, that comment didn't bother me as he meant so little to me. When I look back, I find it very sad that this was all there was between a father and daughter. I knew by then how good father and daughter relationships worked because I saw how my sisters-in-law had caring, loving relationships with their father; but here I was in this hospital with my own, desperately ill Dad, and I resented every minute of it.

I approached him, clutching the bowl of scrambled egg. He looked up through his glasses and said, 'What are they saying? What are they saying about me? Did you get me some fags?' I said that he wasn't to smoke and that he was to eat. 'Look,' I said, avoiding calling him Dad, 'I've got some scrambled egg here. You need to eat if you want to get better.' I put the bowl down on the table in front of his bed, beside the used tissues and little paper cup that he spat into, and tried to coax him to eat. The smell from him was awful, as if he was decaying, and the pallor of his skin confirmed it. He swizzled the eggs around in the bowl with the spoon but didn't eat. I picked up the spoon and, filling it with egg, started to feed him. I didn't really want to – I felt sick doing it, caring for him – but I did have a feeling of obligation. What for, I have no idea.

I got him to eat a bit then I left, saying that I'd be back soon and that he'd better eat while I was gone if he wanted to get better and go home. As I walked back through the green fields of the Meadows, the tears streamed involuntarily down my cheeks. I knew I would have to go back and visit him but I really didn't want to. To see him reminded me of so many bad things in my past and I didn't want to look at those things – or at him for that matter. He was not the person I wanted for a father.

৵

I visited my Dad in hospital on a couple of other occasions. The next time I went, I was approached by a doctor who asked me what my circumstances were, and whether or not I could look after my father at home. I was horrified! Me, look after him in my new clean home with no evidence of my horrible past? I blurted out to this young doctor, 'NO! I couldn't do that, it's completely unthinkable.' I tried to tell him that things had been terrible for me at home when I was a child and that I didn't have that kind of relationship with my Dad, but all of my words became jumbled up and I tripped over what I was trying to say. I'm sure that I must have sounded mad. The doctor could see that I was clearly distressed, so he dropped his suggestions and left me to go back and visit my father. I don't remember much more about that visit, but that conversation with the doctor had shaken me and brought many, many questions into my head about my Dad.

Over the next few days, my thoughts were in turmoil. Images of my past were tumbling over and over in my head, and I was getting increasingly angry about the role my father had played in my childhood. I just knew I had to say something to him. He was ill and worn down, maybe even ready to die, but I just had to ask him what he knew about what Helen had done to me and why, in my eyes, he had never done anything to stop it.

On my next visit to see him, I was armed with the knowledge that this was my opportunity to finally talk to him. My stomach churned and my heart raced as I sat on the number 41 bus on the trip to the hospital. My mind was full of all the questions I would ask – I even went a step further and anticipated his answers. I thought that maybe he would cry (surely he would cry?) and say he was sorry (surely he would say he was sorry?). Maybe he would say that he hated Helen for her actions towards me; maybe he would tell me something about my mother; maybe, just maybe, all the gaps would be filled. Then perhaps we could redeem something.

My optimism didn't last.

When I arrived, my Dad was sitting up in bed, leaning against a mountain of pillows. He told me that he had to sleep like this so that he could breathe. As I watched, he was breathing in and out as if blowing up a balloon. His pyjamas swam around his shrunken frame and he looked very vulnerable. Initially, we just went through some small talk. I gave him a book I had brought for him, a cowboy story. I didn't really know what he liked but I remembered that he loved the old Western movies that were often shown on Sunday afternoons. I arranged the grapes I'd brought him in the little bowl on the locker by his bed, throwing into the bin the uneaten ones from a previous visit. Then, during a lull in our awkward conversation, I just started talking. My head felt as if it was going to explode, my voice shook along with my whole body, but I just started pouring the words out.

'Dad,' I began, 'I need to ask you some things about when I was a child.' At this, he looked straight at me. His eyes seemed huge through his glasses and, as I looked at his worn, thin face, I thought that I wouldn't be able to go on with the questions – but I did. I asked him whether he knew about all the beatings Helen had given me. Did he know about me being starved and locked up? Did he know about the sexual abuse? As I spoke, he put his hand up as if to signal to me to stop and then turned his head away from me.

'Dad,' I pleaded. 'Please tell me – did you know?'

He lay there in that hospital bed with the curtain partially hiding us from the rest of the ward. I could hear the sounds of life around going on – the clip-clop of nurses walking up and down busying themselves with their patients; the sound of the tea trolley being wheeled from bed to bed and cups and saucers clinking as they went. I could hear other visitors chatting to their sick relatives as I stood there waiting for my father to answer me.

I waited and waited and waited.

I begged him over and over again: 'Dad, please tell me! Please tell me!' but he kept his face turned away from me, waving his hand to signal me to be quiet.

'Dad,' I said. 'Please! If you don't speak to me I'm going to go.'

I waited for a bit longer, watching him while the tears welled up in my eyes.

He didn't say anything; he didn't even look at me.

Finally, before I embarrassed myself by crying in front of him, I picked up my bag and left.

I walked up that ward, past all the other patients who were laughing and chatting and hugging with their visitors, and I walked through the long corridors out into the Edinburgh sunshine. I left behind my father and any hope I ever had of him saying sorry, of explaining his role, of explaining about Helen, of telling me anything about my mother.

I walked away from him and I walked away from my past.

I never saw him again.

Chapter Twenty-six

જી

WHAT DADDIES DO

AFTER THIS PARTICULAR STAY IN hospital, my Dad went to live in sheltered housing in the Abbeyhill area of Edinburgh with Karen. It seemed like an odd situation and living environment for such a young girl, but Karen has said that she was glad about where they ended up because it was safer and cleaner than some of the other places they had been living. Up until then they had been in a flat in Rossie Place. That flat had no lock on the front door so it was permanently open to anyone who passed by. Karen was terrified in the evenings as she was usually left there on her own while my Dad was at the pub. One evening, when she was about 10 years old, she was so worried that she ran out into the street at 11pm, crying and screaming, until a neighbour went and got my Dad from Middleton's pub.

Dad was in and out of hospital for the rest of his life. I remember his funeral but, oddly, I don't recall the date of his death, but our relationship had never been traditional.

જી

My father, my flesh and blood, had chosen to be the prime carer for me, taking me home from Barnardo's to nothing more than a life of abuse and neglect. As far as I'm concerned, he was as accountable as Helen or any of the men who violated me because he was my Dad – and fathers are supposed to be protectors, no matter what. They are supposed to love us and nurture us, listen to us and allow us a voice. They are supposed to praise us and instil us with confidence; and they are supposed to protect us. My father didn't do any of these things.

My views of what 'real' fathers did came from a number of places – not just story books and fairy tales, but life and my experiences of it too. While I was in the children's home I had visited a family from time to time on a Saturday or Sunday. I'm not sure where this was exactly but I think it may have been fairly close to the children's home as there wasn't much travelling involved. According to the files from Barnardo's, there had been so little contact from my father at one stage that I was being considered for 'boarding out', which I think may have meant fostering or adoption. I wonder now if these visits to this family had anything to do with this; maybe they were checking to see whether I would fit in or what I was like away from the environment of the children's home.

Anyway, I remember aspects of these visits. I know there was a little girl who lived in this family; she was around my age and called Andrina. What I remember most about going to that house was the way the family all got on with each other. Andrina's Dad would pick her up and throw her in the air while she laughed and screamed with joy. He'd push us both on the swings, laughing and joking with us all the time. Andrina's Mum would be in the background somewhere, either laughing along too, pottering in the garden or cooking the meal we would all sit down to.

This was my very, very first impression of how a Dad should be.

This is what I thought I was going home to when I clutched my own Daddy's hand the day he took me home.

Sadly, my Daddy was very different. He didn't seem to be able to interact with me the way Andrina's father did with her. I saw him play with the boys, tickle them, and even sit them on his knee. When I first returned to Edinburgh, he once or twice did the same with me but I clearly remember Helen telling him not to baby me, so any affection my Dad may have wanted to give me was soon thwarted by whatever was going on in Helen's mind.

I was a five-year-old girl who needed love, affection and reassurance. Instead, I was made to feel that I was not important. I was made to feel unloved. I used to dream about a different life and different parents, and I would cry and cry for my Mummy. I would look at my Daddy, watch him playing with the boys and wish he would see me.

I never felt that he saw me. I held on to the hope that one day he might, and that maybe he did love me as much as he loved them.

࿐

As I grew older, I discovered books that opened up to me another world of how fathers should be. One of my favourites was *Little Women*. When I read the chapter in which Mr March returns from the war just in time for Christmas, I wept and wept, thinking how different life must be for some families. What I would have given for a Daddy like Mr March! Why couldn't my Dad be like him? He was loving and warm to his daughters, in spite of his injuries, so why couldn't I get just a bit of love from my own Dad?

In my adult years, I've met many men whom I would class as being 'good fathers'. These men were the antithesis of my own Dad. They loved their children and showed them this by hugging and nurturing them, listening to them, providing for them, playing with and protecting them. My first important 'fatherly' relationship with a man other than my own Dad was with my first husband Robert's father. The first time Robert took me home to visit his parents, I was bowled over by that family. They were intelligent, kind, caring, smart . . . and they accepted me. I developed very good relationships with both of his parents, although initially I was scared because I didn't know what to expect, having known only my own dysfunctional family life. I was most nervous about meeting Robert's father, Bob Shipman, but I needn't have been as he made me feel comfortable in his presence from the outset.

I can honestly say that this was the single most important relationship with a man I have had in my adult years because it allowed me to shape a real role model of how fathers should be. Through him, I got the father I never really had. It was he who arranged and paid for my wedding to Robert. It was he who was the granddad to my children. He taught me to cook roast dinners; we went to the theatre and concerts; we even went shopping together. Robert and I would join Bob nearly every weekend at his holiday cottage in St Monance. This time in my life was full and rewarding because I finally had the parents and family I'd always wanted.

When Bob died I was devastated. I cried so hard at his funeral. Looking back, his immediate family must have wondered about the intensity of my grief, but, of course, they knew nothing about my past or just how much this man meant to me. Perhaps they will understand if they read this.

∽

Chapter Twenty-seven

MY BOY, MY GIRLS

PAUL WAS BORN ON 26 November 1986. He arrived on the day he was due and weighed exactly 9lb. I'm not a very big person, and Robert isn't very tall either, so it was quite a surprise to give birth to such a big baby; an extremely painful surprise! I felt that Paul was *the* most wanted baby ever. After having suffered a miscarriage the previous year, I felt that I was doomed not to have children. Also, although I never discussed it, I was terrified that the years of sexual abuse had done untold damage.

As I sat in hospital on a very wintry day with my beautiful boy in my arms, I was overjoyed that I had been given such a gift, and terrified that I wouldn't be able to be a good mother to him. I needn't have worried, though, because I couldn't even let him out of my sight. When the nurses came to take him for his heel jab I cried pitifully. I'm sure they must have thought I was a complete lunatic, but only I really knew how very precious this baby was to me.

The first night I took Paul home he slept in a Moses basket right beside my bed and I fed him on demand. I read book after book on how to bring up children and how to stimulate them. My favourite author at the time was Penelope Leach. I bathed him and fed him, sang to him and read him the newspapers. I took him out for walks and showed him the world. At 10 months, he was walking. At a year, he could recite nursery rhymes. By the time he went to school he was reading. Although I'd initially been terrified of letting him down, I actually found motherhood very easy. There were so many rewards just sitting there as I watched him develop and grow. The reassurance that I was doing well came from Paul's happy demeanour and self-confidence.

There have been difficult times, such as when Robert left, and times when he has had to be 'the man' of the family, but I am proud to say that he has turned out to be one of the most well-balanced and likeable young men I have ever had the pleasure to know. Paul and I discuss most things and we have a good relationship. He is warm and kind and a gentleman.

It would have been very easy for me to have overprotected my children or been too soft with them. However, I made a decision early on in Paul's life that I would do the opposite of what happened to me as a child – I would bring them up in a fair environment where they always had a voice. They would be able to question anything I asked of them; and if they felt what I was asking was unfair then they should not be expected to comply just because I said so. I also felt it was important to give them boundaries – bedtimes, manners, respect and so forth.

I love all my children equally and differently. They are my finest achievements in life, but there is something in particular about Paul that gets to me. Perhaps it's because he's a boy and I've had to be both Mum and Dad to him. Maybe the knowledge that the way I've brought him up has paid off enormously is at the bottom of our relationship. Paul knows about my past in general but doesn't know all the details. I'm happy for it to stay that way until he chooses, if ever, to read my story.

Paul is very like his father in both physical appearance and nature, yet I see some of my characteristics in him too – his utter optimism for a start. He has a complete love of life and adventure, meeting people and travelling. There is too much in the world for Paul to see. These are a few of the things that make me very proud of him, and proud of myself for having managed to raise such a lovely boy against all the odds.

࿔

Claire was born in September 1987, and, unlike Paul, arrived three weeks early. She was 6lb 10oz and absolutely gorgeous, with big dark eyes and a shock of black hair. I was much more confident with Claire. I wasn't so worried and didn't have the anxieties I'd experienced when I first brought Paul home. Paul was so lovely with her; there was none of the sibling rivalry that I had read of and expected, even though he was only 18 months old at the time. He was loving and protective of his new little sister – whether this had something to do with the fact that I had got him his own baby doll to look after before she came home, I don't know. We'd bathe our babies together, take them out for walks and read them stories.

Claire was a happy, joyful little girl and determined, very determined. She has been a real joy to me, and has grown into a woman I am very proud of. Even though she struggled at school with dyslexia, she never let it get in her way, and has overcome any problems she may have had to finally land herself a place at university to progress to her much coveted career as a midwife.

She has known loss and rejection, as has Paul, because, sadly, the relationship between Robert and I didn't last. He left when Claire was two and a half. I still care for Robert, and I don't want to say anything about our life together that he may not want to be made public. However, when he left to go and live in Portugal with a new partner some years later, he didn't seem to realise that it was still very important to maintain contact with his children, to reassure them of his love for them and make them feel as important as his new partner. As an adult, I could see that this was because he had wrongly assumed that the children no longer needed him now they were growing up. However, Claire's adolescent mind, rightly so, couldn't understand and saw it as rejection.

Claire and I have had to work through many issues regarding this, coupled with the fact that my second husband also felt threatened by the link between Claire and myself. He tried at all opportunities to divide and separate us, but he could never break the bond that we had established many years before. It is my belief that if you make this bond well with your children in the early years of their lives – if you nurture them, play with them and love them – no-one can ever change that.

Claire is a wise and clever young woman. She could see through my second husband long before I did, but she stuck it out and supported me. When I finally saw for myself the damage and destruction he was trying to create – when I finally plucked up the courage to leave him – it was Claire who was there to see me through it all. Claire has good values; she is headstrong and focused; she is a respectful, loving daughter, a wonderful friend, and – most importantly – she is her own person.

And then there is my baby. Saoirse was born in December 1996, and, as I always say to her, she was the finest, most wonderful Christmas gift I have ever had. I met Chris, her father, before I travelled to South Africa. I liked him from the start as he was a kind and gentle person, the type of man who is everyone's friend. When I returned from my travels, we hit it off, started dating and within no time we were living together. We both needed someone and just fell into each other's lives. Within a matter of months I was pregnant. I couldn't believe it as I was usually so careful about taking precautions, and I wouldn't generally just fall into a relationship so quickly, but I did this time. When I knew I was going to have a baby I was genuinely delighted. For some reason it seemed right.

My children knew Chris. They had always liked him and his

gentle ways. Everything just fell into place, and the result was Saoirse. Her name is the Irish Gaelic for 'freedom'. When she arrived, she was like an angel coming into our lives. She was white blonde from the moment she was born, and still has lovely blonde hair and the bluest eyes. Saoirse is such a gentle, loving girl, with the most beautiful singing voice. She is artistic, insightful and very clever. We all fell in love with her from the moment we saw her. Claire was like a little mum to her and Paul just loved to show her the world.

Chris and I tried to make our relationship work, but, sadly, it didn't. However, he is a wonderful father to Saoirse and remains a respected friend to us all. I would say that Saoirse is the child who has been with me the most on my journey into my past, albeit without her actually knowing. She was only five years old when I gave my statement to the police regarding my stepmother, the same age as I was when I returned to live with my father and Helen. That was very difficult. I looked at my little girl every day as I went through the memories of what had happened to me, and I wondered, as I saw her innocence, how any adult could actually want to damage such purity. I had to keep myself in check all of the time. I had to make sure I didn't overcompensate for my pain and possibly destroy her childhood in the process. I wanted to protect her but didn't want to overprotect her. These issues weren't there in Paul and Claire's childhood because the past then was buried, but every day as I was faced with a new memory, a new pain, it was very difficult to see this child and not think of myself at that age.

I don't know how but I managed to keep it from her. She knew, as my older children did, that something was going on, and I knew I had to give her an explanation. The only way I felt I could explain it to her was by telling her the story of Snow White – I was Snow White and Helen was the evil stepmother. When I finally went to court, I told her that the man (the judge) was going to tell Helen that she had been very bad and that she had to say sorry. With this explanation I was able to simplify and explain in a way that she could understand.

Saoirse is 11 years old now and understands a little more than she did then, but it's not a topic that comes up very often – and I won't allow it to because that was my childhood, not hers. She has a normal, happy life with a Mum, Dad, sister and brother who love her, and a big extended family and many friends. She is a little girl growing and developing in a world far from mine. She is without fear and surrounded by love. I can give her what I never had, and I am so very thankful for that.

Chapter Twenty-eight

৵

OUT OF THE FRYING
PAN . . .

MY SECOND MARRIAGE WAS IN stark contrast to my relationship with, and wedding to, Robert. I met Ian on Saturday 8 July 2001. I was at home in North Berwick, sitting in my living room and having a few laughs with my girls as we got ready to watch *Blind Date*. It was a weekend tradition with us, and we all loved spending that time together, messing about and enjoying each other's company.

The phone rang and a friend said that I should come round to her house as she had someone else there and she thought we'd get along well. I took the girls with me and there he was. Ian. I wasn't deliberately looking for a man; I'd been on my own for a while, with a few unimportant dates here and there. My first impression of Ian, however, was a good one. He was charming and friendly, and we hit it off immediately. Later, he offered to walk us home. He came in, we had a cup of coffee and chatted, and he said he'd like to see me again. I was due to have friends over to visit on the Sunday afternoon and suggested that Ian come along too.

It wasn't exactly a whirlwind relationship, but he was around quite a lot over the next few weeks. Ian was very different from the men I was usually attracted to – he was a lot bigger and less well educated than my previous partners. I think that my attraction to him was entirely physical, and he did have a strong sexual presence. However, the exact same attributes that drew me to him would bring about the downfall of our relationship before long.

It was unusual for me to feel this way. I had never been able to have one-night stands, always needing to feel a connection with a man – usually on some level of intelligence – before I could even contemplate a physical bond. With Ian, I wanted to have the emotional link so that the sexual relationship would flow naturally, but the attraction was so immediate for me that I thought I could forgo my usual pattern this time.

At the time when we met, I was really busy with work. I had taken on a huge job, gutting and renovating the interior of a house in Edinburgh for a very successful music business player. I adored the planning, the liaising with craftsmen and builders, the detailed artistic redevelopment of something beautiful and challenging. I already felt successful and happy. I had my children and my career, and I hadn't looked at my past for a long time.

All that changed without any warning.

~

One day, a few months after I had met Ian, the doorbell rang when I was at home with Paul, Claire and Saoirse. I didn't think about who it could be, and when I opened the door to reveal two police officers, I still didn't connect their presence with anything to do with me. I asked them in – a woman and a man – and they said that they had a few questions for me. I confirmed my name and my date of birth, and then everything started swimming in my head. The police officers said that they had been contacted by my half-brother who wanted to prosecute Helen Ford, our stepmother, for what she had done to us all those years ago. They said that they had Simon's statement, but would like to ask me whether I would also be willing to make one so that the Procurator Fiscal could determine whether the case should proceed.

I was in shock.

My past – which I had tried to stop overwhelming my life since as far back as I could remember – was sitting in front of me. The two officers, who were from the Family Protection Unit of Lothian and Borders Police, were really nice. They told me that there was no rush, that I shouldn't feel forced into anything, and that I should take as much time as I needed before coming to a decision. They sat with me for a while as I tried to take it in, but I really just wanted them to leave so that I could begin to process what they had brought with them.

When they finally did go, saying that they would be in touch again and giving me their contact details, I was stunned. Stunned and nauseous. I wanted to be sick; I wanted to get this out of me – but something kept niggling in the corners of my mind. I knew what they had said; I understood what my options were; but there was something else that was almost taking shape. What was it?

Finally, it came to me.

This meant that people were willing to listen to me. They would listen to my stories of what she had done to me – what they had all done to me – and they would believe me. They had looked for me and they had found me, and now it was up to me to decide whether I wanted to take this to the next stage.

I know for a fact that if that knock on the door had never happened – or even if it hadn't happened *then* – that Ian and I would never had stayed together for any length of time, never mind get married to each other. When I next saw him I told him about the police visit, but gave him as few details as possible. I hadn't mentioned this stuff to him before as I never anticipated needing to. I couldn't go into details; I simply said that my half-brother had accused our stepmother of cruelty when we were children, and that the police had visited to see if I would consider making a supporting statement. I didn't really feel able to say much more as I'd only known Ian since that summer, and this wasn't material I spoke about casually.

The day after the police visited, I went to see my very close friend, Christine, who also lived in North Berwick. Since the day I met her, Christine has been my confidante, my guide and my support. It was a huge thing for me to feel this way about her – I had been abandoned by my mother and the next important female in my life was my abuser, and yet I had always still been able to trust women. Christine had proved to me that I was right to retain that trust, and she kept on giving me help whenever I needed it. She does to this day.

Christine played devil's advocate and said things I needed to hear. She asked how I would feel if I gave a statement but the Procurator Fiscal decided not to prosecute. She asked how I would feel if I was torn to shreds while testifying. She asked how I would feel seeing Helen Ford again. And she asked how I would cope if she was found 'not guilty'. This was all important. She grounded me, but in a supportive way without ever making me feel that she was putting her point of view on everything.

We sat at her kitchen table, constantly drinking cups of tea, and I told her more than I'd ever told anyone before. Places I had never gone were pulled out that day and I wept continuously as I looked back on the child I had been. In the past, I had always just told people that I'd never had a happy childhood and I didn't have any family, and left it at that. With Christine, I faced those stories head-on. I told her what the reality had been. She suggested that I needed to put myself first and think what all of this might do to me. She was right in many ways – sometimes the past is best left there – but she also managed to make me feel empowered by showing me that I did have choices.

I reflected on everything Christine and I had discussed, but I also had to consider my relationship with Ian. His approach was very different from hers.

He wouldn't let it go.

He wanted to know everything, every little detail. What had Helen done to me? What had those men done to me? Where?

How often? How bad was it? How did I feel?

It was relentless and he broke me down with it every time we saw each other.

As I tried to decide whether I wanted to give a statement and be part of a court case, Ian kept telling me over and over again what I *should* do, what I *had* to do, what I *must* do, what I *needed* to do. I felt pressurised every time we spoke about it – and every time we met, we did speak about it because he always wanted to.

When I had been introduced to him, I was independent, self-sufficient and strong. I was a single parent trying to keep my head above water financially, but I was managing. Would I have made the decision to go ahead with the police questioning if I hadn't met Ian? I don't know – I think I would.

Ian was at my house constantly. He lived in a grotty bedsit – in fact, he came to me with nothing at a time when I was in shock. I remember thinking that my head would actually explode, but I was also exhilarated that I might finally get some closure on this period of my life which still haunted me when it could. It was a surreal time as I was being put back into a place I hadn't visited for almost 20 years, not since the death of my father. I had these extreme emotions going on in my head but I also had a normal life to cope with at the same time. I felt that Ian and I were getting on, even though the warning signs were already there, but I also remember very clearly the feeling that things were spiralling out of my control.

৲

After about six months, I knew that I had to do something about the potential court case. The memories that had been triggered had made me very weak. Ian had decided to move in with me, convincing me that it was the right thing to do. I had started feeling incredibly insecure, and had pulled out of the house restoration job as what I was going through was crippling me.

I was beginning to get feelings that were familiar, but I didn't know what they were. I had palpitations and anxiety attacks, and I woke every morning feeling sick. I was right back where I was terrified of going – the place I had avoided for years – and it could only get worse.

Chapter Twenty-nine

FOR BETTER, FOR WORSE

IAN'S RESPONSE TO ALL OF THIS?

He asked me to marry him.

And I said that I would. I know now that I married him for all the wrong reasons. I was desperately seeking security. My world had been turned upside down with the invasion into my past, and I clung to the only person around who seemed to offer me some stability. It would be so easy at this point to blame the disaster of this relationship entirely on him, but I was an adult and I made a conscious decision to become so involved with him that marriage became an option.

By the time I met Ian, Robert and I had been separated for 11 years, yet we were still legally married as neither of us had pursued a divorce. I continued to use his name – to be honest, I had never really wanted to divorce him. I suppose, subconsciously, I always hoped that we would get back together.

I'll be upfront and admit that I really don't have anything nice to say about Ian now that we are apart. He hurt me and scared my children, but I have since tried to make sense of why I allowed him into my life in the first place. I had spent all of my adult life trying to avoid people who would cause me pain and anguish or who would in any way threaten my children, yet here I was not only getting involved with someone who was aggressive and controlling, I had taken it a step further and chosen to marry him. I was clinging to something I thought I was being offered; I didn't want to be on my own at this time; but I still feel so guilty that I chose this man.

He said that we had to move out of the beautiful North Berwick house, and he was really insistent about it. He promised me so much. He said that a new house in which we could start together would be so much better – better for him as it would be in his name and cost half as much as the one I was renting. And it would be further away from Christine. He found us a cottage in Dirleton, north of where I had been living, and it was horrific. The place was a complete mess and I had to gut it.

One day I went there on my own to try and get a room organised for Saoirse. I spent all day in my element, cleaning and stripping it before painting murals on the wall and turning it into a wonderland for my little girl who was only five at the time. It was beautiful and I was really proud to be channelling myself into something positive and loving like that. That night, I took Ian up to see it. I held his hand as we went in and got him to close his eyes so that it would all be a surprise. We walked down the corridor and when we got there, I peeled his hands away from his eyes to show him my handiwork.

He went ballistic.

'You stupid bitch!' he shouted at me. 'What the fuck did you do that for? You can't paint – you've made a fucking mess of the place! How stupid, just how stupid can a person be?' he shouted at me over and over again. Ian was a big man, much, much bigger than me, and as he hollered, he towered over me, terrifying me with his physical presence.

I'd never heard him shout before but I should have heard something else – alarm bells.

I was so upset, and he quickly became apologetic in an over-the-top way, saying that he was sure I wouldn't marry him now and that he had ruined everything. All I saw was this big man in tears, saying that he was sorry over and over again.

I fell for it.

⌘

Another problem was that Ian had a big issue with my older children, Paul and Claire. He had a number of sons with his ex-wives and partners. In fact, he was even a granddad by this time. Nevertheless, he saw fit to tell me how to raise mine. I am enormously proud of my children and always have been. They are good, kind, generous, hardworking people with strong values and a horror of even the thought of any kind of violence, given that I never subjected them to it at any point of their young lives, but Ian was obsessed with telling me that I needed to discipline them. I don't know why, because they never did anything wrong (not that I would have hit them if they had), but he went on and on about it, saying that I was too soft, always trying to drive a wedge between us. I'd never smacked my kids, but one day he slapped Paul, hard, right across the face in front of the others and I saw the looks pass between them. They hated it. They hated him. And I couldn't do anything; I was so scared of him.

I felt powerless because of where I was at. I was going through the motions. I started feeling about Ian the way I felt about Helen. The minute I started having flashbacks, I went off sex completely, and I couldn't stand the feeling of vulnerability when I was naked. He loved having parties, which clearly brought back horrible emotions for me. They were never normal, happy events – they had too much drinking, too much arguing, too much dope. For the first time I had let my barriers down and this was how I had been rewarded.

⌘

Ian never really tried to compensate for the awful times. Even on special, symbolic occasions, he didn't make the effort. I don't believe that you need to throw a lot of cash about to make things nice, but it doesn't take much to make someone feel special. For most of my children's lives, I've been skint, yet I've always taken the time and made the effort to make things wonderful for them. Even with Ian, I tried to make things fantastic. I painted his guitar case with a beautiful Celtic design; I bought him a bodhrán and painted that too. I looked after him, cooking and cleaning for him, and I listened to him. I spent money on clothes and holidays for him and, most importantly, I was always there, always there for him.

It wasn't reciprocated. He took all the words that I had told him hurt me so badly when Helen had used them, and he repeated them over and over again. I couldn't work by this time as I was so incapacitated by the stress and anxiety involved in deciding to co-operate with the police, and he threw that at me whenever he could.

There was always an agenda with Ian. To him, everything was always because of one of my 'problems'.

So, I did it.

I married him.

I know that I was vulnerable. I know now that the warning signs were all there, yet I continued the relationship. I know so much now that it's over.

I would spend time listening to his stories of how bad his life had been, and how people had been so horrible to him. I really, really believed I could change him, like so many women believe they can change so many men. When he said he loved me I believed him, even though there were many incidents of him being involved with other women while we were together, before and after we married. I believed him when he said he was sorry after he had terrified me with his aggression and bullying. I was spiralling into my past and I needed love, support and protection more than at any other time in my adult life, yet here I was faced with a man who offered me the exact opposite. As I've said, I misread all the signals and I chose to marry him.

I was fed up of relationships not working. I didn't want to be on my own any longer, and I did feel a link to him at the start. But this wedding? This wedding would be so very different from my first and I could feel my heart breaking from the start.

ॐ

On the night before the wedding, I stayed at the home of my dear friend Christine and her husband, Stuart. We got married on the August bank holiday in 2002. That suited Ian as it meant all of his English friends could be there. I was late. Thirty minutes before it was due to start, I still hadn't done my hair and I was sewing my dress together. Christine and Stuart had tried to make it special for me. Stuart wrote me a beautiful letter and drove me there; Christine was by my side the whole time, even though she had previously warned me that Ian would never change.

We got married in the garden of a pub in Dunbar that had been Ian's local, and everything was done on a very tight budget. I designed and made my own dress; and we had mince and potatoes for our meal with a grand dessert of spotted dick and custard. We went home on the coach back to North Berwick with all the people who came to the wedding, and then we went back to the house we were living in. I had a very heavy heart that day because I knew instinctively it was all wrong, but by then I'd gone too far down the road to turn around. Unlike the happiness and joy of my first wedding, I was miserable.

Christine had offered to look after the children for me so that Ian and I could get a bit of a honeymoon. The day after the wedding, however, I was incapacitated by a terrible virus. I lost my voice and was too ill to even move.

We were together but there was no romance, no wonderful

moments for me to recall later, and Ian was angry with me all the time because sex was the last thing on my mind. All the time that I was with him, he never once took me out for a nice meal or a romantic date. I let him become part of my life and my children's lives, and he stamped on all of it.

It would be so easy to blame what I was going through for the troubles we had throughout this relationship. However, when I had later dealt with most of my past and was coming out the other side, I devoted a great deal of time and energy into trying to resolve what Ian called my 'issues'. I attended six sessions at Relate where I spoke at length about what we had been going through, and I accepted that some of this may have been directly related to my past – but I knew also that a great deal of it had to do with the person he was. On the seventh session, Ian came along to allow me to face him in a safe environment but it was disastrous. Neither of us went back to Relate. There was no point. I just needed to get out.

༄

Chapter Thirty

ESCAPE

LEAVING IAN WASN'T EASY.

I had often thought about it but it always seemed such an enormous task. I moved with him to his home town 300 miles away from Edinburgh, thinking that if we got away from everything, we might have a chance to repair our damaged relationship. I also thought that the move might give him a chance to develop bonds with the sons he'd had with other women, and that this might make him more receptive to my children. In reality, I ended up exactly where he wanted me – isolated and, to begin with, without a single friend to call on. I kept trying to make it work between us, although my heart was always heavy and I didn't trust him. Ironically, the final catalyst for our split came about through Ian's own doing.

I treated myself to a holiday to India to meet up with my niece Hannah. She'd gone there for a six-week trip and had asked me to join her. I hadn't been on holiday on my own in many years and, after all I'd been through, I decided to allow myself this time out. I thought that if I had some time away from Ian, I might come back refreshed, and this would give us a good starting point from which to move forward. My friend Saritha looked after Saoirse for me for the two weeks, and I had a wonderful time. We travelled from Delhi to Goa then to Mumbai, down to Rajasthan, up to Agra to see the Taj Mahal then back to Delhi where we spent the last few days. On my way home I was absolutely elated, and so excited about seeing my girls. I had even missed Ian. I was optimistic, refreshed and the happiest I had been for a long time.

My happiness was soon shattered. After spending time with everyone, giving them the presents I'd bought and telling them all about my trip, I opened my mail. In among all the usual post there was a letter. On opening it, I discovered a Valentine's card addressed to someone else but in Ian's writing. It was signed by him and there was a love note inside. I knew of this person – this woman – from his past, and I knew that he had sent it to her; she, in turn, had seen the sense to send it to me.

I was devastated. He vehemently denied it, immediately getting defensive and accusing people of trying to come between us. The only person who was coming between us was him. I couldn't speak to him. I was hurt and angry. I felt utterly betrayed yet again. Things were silent between us for days. He tried to reassure me but this was the straw that broke the camel's back. I just couldn't take any more. I knew I had to get out – I just didn't know how. I had to hatch a plan to get Ian out of my life.

I suggested to him that he have a holiday visiting his sister in the States. I offered to pay for the trip, saying that since I had been on a break maybe he too would like one. I even suggested that it might give us time to think. He took me up on my offer. I confided in Claire and told her that I needed to get away from him. She was overjoyed that I had finally made the decision.

That this was the right move was further confirmed when he blew a fuse one morning before his trip to America and flew into the most aggressive rage ever. I ran to tell Claire to keep out of the way as he was on the warpath. As he poured himself a huge measure of vodka, I stood by the phone threatening to call the police if he didn't calm down. He left – drunk, in his car. When we finally spoke that evening, once Saoirse was safely tucked up in bed, I was adamant with him that I wanted out. I don't think he believed me because he acted as if nothing had happened and nothing had been said. I just let it go because it was easier, and I knew that my plans to leave were still going to happen.

A few days later, I dropped him off at the airport for his trip, and no sooner was he away than I headed for Edinburgh with the girls. I quickly found a flat for us, and then went back down south. Within two weeks we had packed up all our belongings, said our goodbyes to the couple of friends we did have there, and departed for my home city to start our lives over again without fear and aggression threatening us every day.

⌇

The first few months after I returned were both good and bad. It was good because I was finally away from Ian and I felt free for the first time in ages. But I was also fearful that he would find us. He was constantly texting and phoning me until I changed my number. The stuff he said and alleged was just horrible – I don't think I'd realised how twisted he was until that moment.

I was lost, too, because it had been a long time since I'd made my own decisions. I was hurting very badly, although not in the same way that I did when Robert and I split. I was hurting because I had made the decision to be with this man who had nearly destroyed not only me but my children too. I had given him so much but all he seemed to want was to control us and destroy the safe family unit I had created. With the loving support of my family – my children, nieces, nephew, sisters and brothers-in-law – and my very good friends, I have managed to come through it all. Now, two years down the line, I can honestly say I have turned a corner. I know it wasn't long before Ian got himself another partner who now lives with him in the house we once shared.

I wake up alone. But feeling safe.

Over the time since I have been away from Ian, I have questioned how I could have allowed myself to get into such a destructive relationship. I can't change the fact that it happened. What I can take from it is an enormous lesson, and I can be grateful that I had the courage and wherewithal to get away from him and his ways before he did any more damage. I haven't bottled it up and allowed it to damage me more; I have been allowed to talk about it and see it all clearly.

It's not dark any more.

Chapter Thirty-one

ॐ

A WORLD OUT THERE

I LOVE TO TRAVEL. It's always been a priority for me to see as many countries as I can and to introduce my children to different worlds because it's an education as well as an opportunity to rest and relax. We've never had much money but I've always had belongings that I would easily sell to give us the opportunity to go and see other parts of the world. My children laugh now at the fact that they would arrive home from school and ask, 'Where's the sofa?' and I would reply, 'I sold it – but we're going on holiday!' Off we'd go somewhere hot where we could soak in the ambience and culture. There was a time in Crete when we ran out of money towards the end of our holiday. I went down to the promenade and did drawings of people so that we could enjoy our last few days there in style.

As a result of this approach, we've seen parts of the world that some people only dream of. Some of these journeys have also been, for me, profoundly moving and almost spiritual times, and as an artist a wonderful opportunity to record the sights I've seen.

In 1995, the year of Nelson Mandela's inauguration, I took Paul and Claire off to South Africa. I had a friend in North Berwick who came from there, and having visited with her the previous spring, I felt strongly that I wanted to spend more time in that beautiful, diverse country, and that my children should come along too. To fund it, I held an exhibition at Belhaven Brewery, who sponsored me and sold enough pieces to give us our tickets and enough money to live on for months. We headed off, full of excitement.

We landed in Johannesburg and travelled by coach during the night to Cape Town. We stayed in the centre in Queen Victoria Straat, opposite the museum and the Botanic Gardens, through which you can reach the presidential home. The sights, sounds and colours of this amazing city were awe-inspiring, and we mixed with all races on our stay here.

After some months, Paul and Claire returned on their own to live with their father and go back to school, while I stayed on to complete some work that had been commissioned. I had never been separated from my children for longer than a couple of weeks, so it was very traumatic to see them off at the airport. I thought my heart was going to break, and I truly wondered how I could survive for the few months that I'd be without them. However, I'd never before had an opportunity to follow my own path, and I selfishly allowed myself this one time.

I moved out of Cape Town to a little place called Simon's Town. On nearby Boulders Beach, visitors have to share the sand with the jackass penguins, so-called because of their distinctive donkey-like call. I lived in an old farmhouse high on the hill in the south end of the town. Here I was able to draw and paint and find the peace and solitude I needed so badly. I'd hardly ever been on my own as an adult, basically because I was scared of being so. I'm sure this had much to do with spending so much time on my own as a child, locked up in my boxroom. Here in this wonderful environment, however, I was able to enjoy a peace I had never before known.

I spent many hours outdoors studying the wildlife. I'd watch porcupines sauntering slowly across the fields until they were suddenly threatened by baboons with ferocious yellow teeth. For what seemed like hours, I'd stand watching the schools of porpoises chase the tuna in the Atlantic Ocean. Sometimes I would just walk and think, contemplating my life and the direction it should take next. I often thought about the past and what had gone on, but I never dreamed that one day I would be sitting here telling my story. I was happy enough to have been given this opportunity to spend some time so very far away from everything I'd known.

The old Dutch-style farmhouse I lived in had white walls and an open porch with a little fenced garden. A couple of cows that belonged to the man in the next house would spend most of the day lolling in the garden. I would often sit there and draw them, but sometimes I would walk around the extensive grounds, past the old ruins which were at one time part of an even bigger, grander farmhouse building.

One day, when I was walking through these grounds, I spotted a piece of paper at my feet. Picking up the folded and yellowing sheet, I discovered that it was a horoscope that had been written many years before. The writing was flowery and of another age, beautifully set out with pen and ink. It was written for someone born on 18 June 1913, not exactly the same date as my own birthday but a Gemini all the same. For me at that moment it was like a message sent from someone somewhere. I looked all around for other signs of life among the rubble and weeds in this area, but there was nothing. Why this letter should have been at my feet at this time in my solitude I will never know, but it was. I read the lines over and over again, and some of the words leapt out at me:

In business life there is indication of change – many changes: such is your destiny, for your nature demands, subconsciously, a change of scenery. To travel is your lot – and if it is not possible to practically exercise this trait, then

> *your reading should be arranged in order to preserve your*
> *personality whole – i.e. read books about travel . . .*

As I read on, I could almost hear Auntie Nellie talking to me in her school-marm Edinburgh accent:

> *The golden rule is, of course, to do something about it – even*
> *if it is only a bus-ride.*

My rational-thinking adult self tells me that it is purely coincidence that I found this letter, but it was as if this small faded piece of paper was talking directly to me. Although the letter was long-winded at times and used old-fashioned language, it still spoke to me. As I read on, it became clear that it had been written by a man:

> *It is a fact that several women have proved themselves better*
> *than men in certain branches, but I have noted that such*
> *people eventually 'de-feminise' themselves through repression*
> *of natural biological instincts.*

These parts made me laugh. However, other parts spoke to me more directly:

> *You cannot possibly give of your mental or intellectual best*
> *unless you are spiritually settled.*

This line summed everything up for me. Life is about looking after all areas of our well-being. We can have great careers and good family lives, but we also need to take care of the not-so-obvious parts of us that need attention. I didn't know back then – sitting on a rock in the African sun reading these words from a time long gone – how I could look after and heal the parts of me that were broken and damaged, but I knew they were there because it was hard for me to find peace. Now, after all these years and the journey I have travelled telling my story, I understand so much more clearly.

჻

Chapter Thirty-two

BREDA

AFTER THE PUBLICATION OF *The Step Child*, there was one question asked by everyone – including me. What had happened to Breda? Where was my mother?

It wasn't until I was in my forties that I was able to find out anything concrete about my biological mother. That only came about because I received my files from Barnardo's prior to the court case against Helen Ford.

From these files I learned that Breda was born on 3 May 1935, and that she used a different name on my birth certificate and those of my older half-brother and half-sister. On my birth certificate she is named as Brenda Ford, although she was never legally married to my Dad. It was noted that she was also known as Breda or Bridie. A letter to my maternal grandmother dated 31 January 1961 queries my mother's true name and states:

> . . . we find that the children's birth certificates give different versions of your daughter's Christian names. Will you please help us over this and let us have by return of post, a letter telling us exactly what are your daughter's Christian names.

A letter from my maternal grandmother in reply, dated 2 February 1961, says:

> *In reference to your letter regarding my daughter's names I would like to state that her Christian names are Bridget Mary.*

So at least I was able to find out her birth name, even though she always seemed like Breda to me. I also discovered from the files that Breda had two older brothers, and that they and my maternal grandparents lived in Kent at the time we were taken into the care of Barnardo's. Although this was, again, meagre information, it was more than I'd ever known as a child. What I didn't like reading, though, were the comments written about her. I knew my mother had left us – I'd been told this many times as a child. What shocked me, though, was that reading about my mother's character was almost like hearing Helen's words pounding in my ears. The words leapt from the page:

> *Lapsed Catholic; the mother bore a very bad character; was suspected of associating with many men.*

This was my mother being spoken about. She was only 26 years old at this point and had three children under five by different fathers. She had been legally married to only one of these men, my older half-brother's father.

The files go on to say how my Dad was working down in Kent with a view to us all possibly settling there. While he was away he had heard through the grapevine that my Mum was 'carrying on' behind his back:

> *He paid a surprise visit to her home in Edinburgh, and found several women occupying the premises as well as the mother. After a somewhat hysterical scene the mother walked out*

with her women friends, and has not been seen since. At this
time the three children were in the City Hospital suffering
from whooping cough.

So that was it – as much information as I could manage to get
regarding my mother.

I couldn't leave it there.

I tried to make sense of it all. I felt outraged at what was written
in these files because it seemed so biased and one-sided. I didn't
want to think this was a true depiction of my mother because in
many ways it sounded so like Helen's version of her. When it came
to writing about Breda in *The Step Child* I tried to be objective. I
didn't want to write this version of her down in black and white
because I still believed in the fairy tale I had created of her, of the
woman my older half-sister had told me about who had lovely
dark hair and was so pretty. I wanted to believe in the version that
my half-brother had told me of the woman who sat and played
with us on the lawn making daisy chains.

I tried to look at her circumstances – this young girl who had
come over from Ireland on the boat with her older brother,
abandoning the strict Catholic upbringing of her life in Tipperary
to find freedom in Britain. At that point I could only speculate
about what kind of woman she may or may not have been. No-
one from her side of the family had ever contacted us in all of the
years I was growing up. No-one ever came along to find out if we
were being well looked after or, indeed, to tell us about Breda or
own lives.

⌇

In 2006 I visited Ireland with my then husband. It was a sad and
weary trip because I knew I was looking for some evidence of my
mother but that it was unlikely I would find any. I was also in a
relationship I was struggling to hold on to. Everything seemed

dark and dreary from the moment I set foot on the ferry from Stranraer to Belfast. The cold, wet day matched my mood. There were very few passengers and it seemed as if we had the whole place to ourselves. On top of that, the ferry was old and worn, and I could almost imagine my mother's own journey over the Irish Sea to her new life all those years ago.

I went to many places in Ireland, from Belfast to Dublin, over to Galway then down to Tipperary, where I stopped off to look around. I wandered through the streets of Tipperary, and even looked around the Catholic graveyard I came across, searching the graves for the name 'Curran', and thinking I could maybe get a glimpse of some evidence of my ancestral heritage. I found nothing to suggest my family had ever been there. On our way to Tipperary, we'd stopped off in the town of Carrick for a spot of lunch – soup and soda bread. I didn't know then that it was indeed here that my mother had once lived, gone to school and grown up.

I came back from that trip to Ireland saddened because I'd found nothing. The only highlight had been in Galway where I'd met a lovely fisherman called Michael. He came from the Connemara area north of Galway and still fished in the round coracles of ancient times. He told me that, without even knowing my story, he thought by my dark colouring that I seemed very Irish, and I reminded him indeed of a Connemara girl.

༄

By the end of the year in which *The Step Child* was published, I was again intent on finding out more about my mother. Who was she, where had she gone and where was she now? Breda has always been the missing piece of the big jigsaw that is my life. I went through the files time and again, looking for anything at all that could point me in her direction. Had I missed something first time round? I hoped so. I finally settled on trying to see if I could contact Breda's brother. I knew roughly where he was because my older half-brother had been in touch with him, but I hadn't been given a contact number for him. So, getting his name, I set about trying to find him.

Linda, who has written the books with me, used her journalistic contacts to try and track him down. Meanwhile, I searched through the phone book for people with his surname and initial in the area where he'd lived when he was mentioned in the Barnardo's files all those years ago.

You can maybe imagine my utter surprise when the first call I made from the extensive list turned out to be his number. Finally, I'd managed to track down an actual surviving relative of my biological mother! I was so excited. However, I was utterly dumbfounded by my uncle's reaction. I had hoped for at least some welcome; maybe for a bit of an insight into where my mother might have gone after she left us. I would have been more than grateful for any information, but it was not to be.

It transpired that my uncle had read *The Step Child*, and he was furious. He had even contacted the publishers and was angry, very angry, that I had 'decried' his family. I had never set out to hurt anyone by telling my story. I told only the truth as I knew it. I speculated over what might have happened to my mother; over what kind of woman she may have been. I tried as best as I could to be as objective as possible in the given circumstances. My uncle told me that I was wrong in my assumptions and that he was prepared to sue me over what he saw as defamation of his family.

But that was never what I had set out to do.

I had been abandoned by my mother at a very early age. Not one thing I had read about her was good, nor did I hear a good word spoken about her by others, and she never came back. I gave her the benefit of the doubt despite all of that. My uncle went on to say how they were a close-knit, loving family, and that had he known what we had been enduring he would have taken us in. What futile words! In light of what happened his words meant nothing – if this family had even scraped the surface of what was going on, they would have seen what our lives were like. We were all deprived of not only a mother but also a gran, grandad, aunties, uncles and cousins. My uncle declared that he had heard nothing of my mother since the 1960s, which also leads me to question the closeness of the family bonds.

He promised to contact me again. He never has, and that is that I suppose. He never once asked how I was, how I was coping; never once said how sorry he was and how he would make it up to me by bringing me into the family who now knew that I existed.

ॐ

I hired a private detective to try and find out any little thing about my mother, yet still nothing turned up. She had gone, disappeared it would seem off the face of the earth. Did she change her identity? Did she die? What on earth happened to her? I don't know – and may never know – the answers to these questions. What is evident is that she had a family – three little children – that she just decided she no longer wanted to be a mother to.

I can't remember ever having a mother. My earliest memory is of living in an institution with many other children in the same position as me, with families who visited sporadically. I had no real sense of who I was or where I belonged. Bizarrely, it was Helen herself who brought the question of my own mother into my head. It was from her that I first heard any reference to my 'real mother'. It was not in any way a nice reference as it came in the form of her screaming abuse at what a whore Breda was and how I was her 'bastard' child, but it made me start missing my Mummy. I can recall watching Helen lavish love and attention on her firstborn, singing and cooing to this little boy, while, in complete contrast, she would shout and scream at me and hit me.

What I felt from her was utter hatred. I wonder now if her hatred of me stemmed from her jealousy over my mother.

When I was little and suffering abuse, I would cry for this elusive Mummy. I would weep and sob and wish that she would come and take me away, and love and protect me like other mothers did their children. On a few occasions I asked my Dad about his ex-lover, but he was always reluctant to give me any information other than that she was Irish. This fact was backed up by the records left behind by my Mum – Irish rebel tunes such as 'The Wearing of the Green' and 'Danny Boy' on black plastic vinyl. Dad would occasionally play these on the old record player. This would often cause an argument, with Helen accusing him of missing 'the cow'. My Dad would, of course, deny this, claiming only to enjoy the tunes.

I no longer miss her. I wouldn't know what to say now if I was ever to meet her. I would still like the opportunity to find out more about my heritage and medical history – birthrights that many take for granted. I would even like to give her the opportunity to tell me her side of the story because, like us all, she too has a story to tell. But it seems as if fate has decided it is a story I will never hear.

Chapter Thirty-three

ॐ

STRENGTH, BLAME AND FORGIVENESS

THE LIFE AND EXPERIENCES I described in *The Step Child* – and now in this book – are not the sum total of all that has happened to me. Like everyone, my story can't be distilled into a few easy chapters. Unlike most people, the story of my childhood was a horrific one, but few stories end at childhood. As I left my wicked stepmother and her world behind, I did not enter a fairy-tale life. The past has left its mark on me – the years of starvation as a child have left me with an eating disorder; the years of beatings on an almost daily basis have left me with constant and agonising back pain; the years of sexual abuse have left me afraid of intimacy and at odds with my own sexual feelings; and the years of loneliness and neglect have left me constantly seeking connections, making me vulnerable and susceptible. Exploring what happened to me as a child, and trying to understand the after-effects, brings with it a freedom – the memories no longer haunt me. To get to that point, I have had to delve into not just my years with Helen Ford, but also my teenage and adult lives, where additional horrific memories have surfaced since my first book was published.

People often ask me how I am so strong and why I am so forgiving. I am strong because I have to be. I must sink or swim

– and I choose to swim. I know that what I endured as a child damaged me and had a direct influence on my adult relationships, but I have only just discovered that by exploring the past and the damage I can deal with it once and for all. As for forgiving, I feel that it isn't my place to forgive the people who committed the crimes against me. Can they forgive themselves? Do they sleep at night? Does the violation of a child and the twisted methods used by these people warrant forgiveness? Why should I, as a person whose whole life has been contorted by the sick yearnings of a very disturbed group of people, forgive? Could you? I've lived my adult life trying to understand my sexual needs and those of the partners I've been with. For most of the time, my life has been clouded by very bad memories, memories of men forcing me as a young girl to pleasure them while constantly telling me that I liked it. Do you know what? I never, ever liked it. I hated it. It wasn't normal. It isn't normal. It's sick and perverse and it was only ever about them.

I was always vulnerable as a child, and I was put in that situation by Helen. Although I don't often think about what she did to me and why she did it, I see it all much more clearly now than when I was standing in the High Court in Edinburgh facing her. Back then, in 2003, I was still that little girl she had tormented and abused. I was so scared of facing her, and when I did she managed to make me feel just as frightened as when I was a child. But now – sitting here safely, having reclaimed my birth name for the first time in many years – I can see Helen Gourlay Ford for exactly what she was, for what she was doing to us and what she herself was getting from it. I have no desire whatsoever to concern myself with what made her like that. Wouldn't it just be so easy to blame it on childhood traumas? Wouldn't it be so easy if she could just say that she was abused as a child? That would be so wrong – so insulting to everyone who was ever hurt as a child but who has fought to be a good person and break the cycle.

≁

Dangerous men and women lurk everywhere. The world is a difficult place for children who aren't protected and loved, and we must all – whether parents or not – look out for little ones, always. I have already told of how Helen left our lives that New Year, but she had also left my father for a few weeks shortly after the birth of Karen. I was overjoyed but missed Karen terribly. The house was buoyant and my Dad seemed all right about Helen's departure – apart from when he'd had a drink, when all he spoke about was getting her back. My Dad constantly made excuses for her. He would say she had 'women's troubles' and use the phrase 'when your Mum gets back', never knowing what wrath would be brought down on me had I ever dared to call her that.

In files dated 10 February 1971, the social worker's report on a home visit states: 'Mr Ford explained that his wife was not at home; they had had a row and she left three weeks ago taking the baby with her.' In this same report it states: 'Donna was one of the reasons for the increasing number of rows Mr and Mrs Ford had been having. Mrs Ford complained that Mr Ford never punished Donna.' That was a laugh.

My Dad was going out quite a bit to Middleton's pub and to the bowling club at that time. On some of these nights he brought a friend back, a local guy with a wife and two children. Henry was a really nice man and so lovely to me – to start with. He brought me sweets and made sure that my Dad got to bed when he rolled home drunk from the pub. This helped me a lot as that was my responsibility in Helen's absence.

My Auntie Nellie had given us a piano some time ago that was gathering dust in the boys' room. One night, my Dad came back from the pub and said that 'Uncle' Henry was going to start giving lessons – to me, only me. I was delighted as I really wanted to learn to play the piano. I had plinked it a few times but the thought of being able to play real tunes on it was so exciting.

A little while after this announcement, my Dad came back from the pub during afternoon closing hours with Henry. They sat chatting for a while and then my Dad, as always, fell asleep. 'How d'you fancy a piano lesson then, Donna?' Henry asked over the sound of my Dad's snoring. I jumped at the chance. Helen had been away for only a little while and here was the evidence that things could change – for the better, I assumed. Henry gave the boys some money to go and get sweets then took my hand to follow him into their bedroom to begin the lesson. I was absolutely brimming with excitement as he sat down at the piano. He was a small, balding man who always seemed to be ready to burst out of his shirt at any minute. He had a huge beer belly and always smelled a bit of body odour which he tried to mask with aftershave – unsuccessfully.

'Jump up here onto my lap,' he said as soon as he sat down. 'You're too wee to sit on the stool.' So I did.

As you read this, I want you to remember that Helen had only been away from my life for a couple of weeks and I was experiencing freedom for the first time. I had been eating food and there had been no parties since she left. Things were the best they had ever been, and here was a man who was always nice, helping to teach me how to play the piano.

But I'd no sooner jumped on his lap, eagerly hitting the keys, than his hand shot straight between my thighs. I tried to jump down but his left hand went around my waist and I just couldn't get away from him. He kept saying 'pretty girl, pretty girl' to me. I can't remember now how I did get away or how long we were there. I just remember the stinging pain and the humiliation of the whole situation. This man came and stayed over at our house for two weeks at one point after falling out with his wife, and although I tried at all costs to avoid him I didn't always manage it. He is probably in his seventies now. I know where he lives. I have friends who know him and know where he drinks. Maybe if he reads this he too will know who he is. I have survived it but

I do wonder how many lives he wrecked in pursuit of his pleasure, and how many more people he violated. How does he sleep at night?

After a little while – far too little – Helen came back and things resumed as they had been before she left. During the time she was away, I had a small glimpse of how things might be if she stayed away, despite the abuse I was still suffering. My Dad didn't lock me up in my room or make me stand for hours in the bathroom – and there were no parties. It was like a holiday away from her. I just wished that she would stay away.

ॐ

I believe that it is so important to tell your story, no matter how difficult it is or how long it takes to be heard. Now is the time to tell the tale of what happened to me as I tried to find the woman I wanted to be, the woman who was hidden within the child locked in the cellar. I need to reflect on how far I have come. I know that the negative relationship experiences I have suffered are a direct link from my past, and that I must rebuild myself by looking at what happened to me and then moving on. I have had to let certain memories into my life – but it is now time to let them go. The search for my mother turned up no new leads, and the publication of my first book led only to negative responses from my remaining family. So – where do I go now?

Chapter Thirty-four

ॐ

A BEGINNING FROM
MANY ENDINGS

RECENTLY, IT WAS MY SON Paul's 22nd birthday and we celebrated it like we do all birthdays in our house – together as a family. We always have a homemade cake and we all join in preparing a meal. This time, we made Japanese food as Paul's fiancée is half Japanese and she showed us how to make sushi. We bought gifts and cards for Paul and we showered him with love.

I remember having a birthday party in the children's home, just a month before I left. It was a happy occasion, made even happier by the thought that my Daddy would soon be coming to take me home to my real family and my new Mummy. I remember getting a nurse's outfit with a striped dress, white hat and apron. There was even a little plastic watch pinned to the front of the apron. That's the only birthday I remember in my childhood. I don't know what happened to the nurse's outfit because when I came home to stay with my Dad and Helen, I had no toys at all.

I don't usually think about the fact that my birthdays were so different from those of my children. This is yet another aspect of my life that was just so wrong and it hurts. Sometimes, however, the past comes back to me when I least expect it, such as on

Paul's birthday. Seeing my children and Ayumi laughing as we all attempted to roll sushi – and Saoirse's face lit up by the candles on the cake that Claire had made – I thought about the contrast between my life and theirs. Of course, I'm ecstatically happy to see how different my children's lives are from my childhood, but sometimes I still weep for the little girl I was. It's strange, but the memory of little details like birthdays can be more hurtful than thinking about the physical, sexual or emotional abuse. I was always alone as a child; I never felt that I belonged; and to not even have a birthday or a Christmas was terrible.

꒰

Throughout my adult years I've questioned many aspects of my personality. I've looked at just how what I endured as a child has affected the woman I've become. Some areas of my life have been rewarding – such as parenting and art – because they were easy for me to grasp. It was, in my eyes, so easy to be a good mother because I knew how it felt to be unloved, uncared for, abused and starved. I knew that I only had to listen to my children's needs and respond to them; I only had to respect and love them and always protect them.

My children have always known that I have a great sense of fun, and we've used every opportunity to enjoy ourselves. They would often come home from school to discover that we'd be having a picnic tea down on the beach or up in the hills. Every morning I woke them with a song – I still do it now with Saoirse, in spite of her telling me I'm out of key! Our house has always been somewhere for my children and their friends to congregate. Whenever I can give them fun I will, but my children have always had boundaries, such as regular mealtimes and bedtimes, because I believe we all need a certain amount of routine to allow us to accept the discipline we need in our adult lives. I have insisted on them having good manners because rudeness is ugly. I am no different from many parents in that I just want the best for my children. The only thing that sets me apart from many is that I had such a terrible example of parenting set for me by my own father and Helen.

My art has always been with me. I just knew in my heart that one day I would be an artist. When I started truanting from school at around the age of 13, I sometimes went to the National Gallery on the Mound to keep warm. Here a world opened up for me. I was blown away by the paintings. I'd stare in awe at the Botticellis, Rembrandts and MacTaggarts, to name a few, and I'd wonder just how they were created. I knew then that one day I would find out.

It took me until I was 30 before I started on my path as an artist, after my marriage to Robert had broken up and I was at a very low point. I decided then to go to college to study art, and although I haven't done everything in the way I would have liked, I am happy because I feel successful. There are many ways that we measure success as an artist. For some, it is enough to sell the odd painting here and there; while other artists would argue that unless you are truly recognised and displayed in the major galleries then success is not yet won. For me, I paint and draw because I love it and because my work brings pleasure to other people. I have exhibited and sold in the UK and abroad, particularly South Africa. Many people have bought my work and are respectful of my achievements. To me, that is success. I do have further hopes and ambitions as far as being an artist is concerned, and I intend to pursue every one of them, but I am delighted with the relative success I now enjoy. Art has always been an escape for me, the one thing that nobody could ever take from me.

꒰

I would say that my major problem in life has been my inability to sustain and nurture relationships with men. I have thought long and hard about this, and I have often wondered just how much what happened to me as a child has had a bearing on my role in personal relationships. There have been four important relationships in my life and I value each one for what it has brought me, but I wish with all my heart that I'd had one and only one, because I believe that families should stay together. I know that break-ups are sometimes unavoidable, and that many single parents do a fantastic job, but I really do believe that it is better for everyone to stay together.

When I was around 15, I started going to the local youth club. One of my friends at this time was a happy-go-lucky, popular girl who had lots of friends, both male and female. I always wished that I had her confidence because she was happy and fun to be around. For her, it was the most natural thing in the world that boys fancied her, and to flirt and have fun with them. I, on the other hand, was terrified of boys coming near me at all. I felt dirty and used, and I thought that boys would know straight away. Although this was the mid-1970s, attitudes in our neighbourhood were still very much stuck in the 1950s when sex before marriage was taboo, and 'nice' girls didn't let boys near them sexually. Another friend of mine who got pregnant, unknown to me, was whisked off to stay with an aunt, returning some months later with a baby.

People who know what it's like to have their innocence stolen will understand what I'm trying to say here. For those who haven't experienced sexual violation in childhood, I would like to explain. When we are children, we don't have much choice. We are ultimately at the mercy of the people who care for us or are involved in our lives. Sometimes these people do terrible things, like my stepmother did, and as did the men who, in their sick depravity, took from me my innocence for their own sexual gratification.

My first important relationship was with Robert. For the first time in my life I was a sexual being. I could give and receive love and know that sex wasn't something that was just taken from me. This feeling was very new as I had previously only known invasion into my secret private places. But when I met Robert, what shocked me was the natural way we enjoyed each other.

We really loved each other in those early days, but we were so very young and we both carried baggage. Unfortunately, at some point in our relationship, life got on top of us. Something had to go and we parted. So many times I look back and think if only I knew then what I know now, maybe we could have stood a chance. I know so much more about how I was damaged and how that would have a bearing on any relationship. If I could go back there armed with that knowledge and wisdom, I believe we could still be together.

I'm not exactly sure when we started having problems but I do remember arguments about why I was no longer interested in sex. I can remember that we were having many difficulties because Robert's business was not succeeding. I was juggling working in the Social Work Department with bringing up two children under five. On top of that, my father-in-law, whom I loved and respected, had a stroke and was paralysed. It seemed like my world was falling apart. I blamed myself and felt that all this bad luck was down to me being rotten inside. I just didn't want sex, and the very thought of it took me back to dark places in my childhood. Rather than dealing with this problem and others that we were having, I just let Robert walk away.

I was heartbroken, and I'm sure Robert was too, but neither of us seemed to have the ability to address any of the real issues we were experiencing. To be perfectly fair, nobody knew what had gone on for me. People have always thought that I am strong and capable of bouncing back, but inside I was a broken little girl trying to deal with the aftermath of many years of abuse, and I didn't know how to cope with the adult world.

As I sit here now it is easy to be melancholic about the past and those times. It is also easy to blame myself or what happened to me as a child for my inability to sustain a relationship, but I know that it takes two people to make a relationship and two people to break it. After Robert and I split, my self-esteem and confidence shattered, and I felt really down about my situation. I had to pick myself up, brush myself down and start again. This was not an easy thing to do because I really believed at this point that I was tainted and inadequate.

Looking back at other relationships, I now know that all the elements must be right for two people to enjoy a healthy sex life. My second marriage was a violent, abusive, controlling one. Ian's idea of sex was about having 'his' needs met. He would bring up my past, and accuse me of being frigid. He broke my nose, terrified the life out of me and my children and then wondered why I couldn't love him in the way he wanted. In the end, I could only have sex with him if I'd had a few drinks.

The relationship with Ian took me to a very bad place. All the time I was with him I was reminded of my past. Having read some psychology I know that this was subconsciously what I expected. With Ian, I knew what to expect all the time. I was always frightened, and that was a feeling I was used to, even though I hated it. I believed that he loved me because he would cry, apologise and tell me that he loved me, and that nobody would ever love me like he did. Everything about his behaviour was wrong and he took advantage of my vulnerability.

That's not love. That's abuse all over again.

⁂

Chapter Thirty-five

Breaking the Silence

IT WOULD BE FOOLISH TO say that I wasn't affected by what happened to me as a child because it is widely recognised that sexual abuse in childhood has a lasting effect. There are many symptoms, some of which I have experienced myself, such as anxiety, panic attacks, nightmares and flashbacks. For some people, sexual abuse leaves them with shame, self-hatred and depression. The betrayal of trust that we experience as children can leave us feeling uneasy in relationships as adults. Some people may cope with these feelings by overuse of drink or drugs. Others may overeat or starve themselves, or self-harm to express the terrible pain and confusion sexual abuse leaves us with. But *it is* possible to get over these feelings. For me, I can overcome a lot of these effects by talking about them – on my terms.

Talking about it breaks the secrecy and allows us to let out the hurt and shame. It helps us see who is really to blame, and rebalances our thoughts about the thing that happened to us that we had no control over. Talking about what happened to me has been the most valuable way of overcoming the anxiety and fear I was left with. I spoke a lot with my good friend Linda, who has helped me write my books. I had spoken to a policewoman about much of it when I gave a statement to the police, but Linda was really the first woman friend I poured my heart out to. I am so grateful that I chose her, and for her sensitivity, because through being able to talk about it and be supported, I have managed to exorcise many of my demons.

Since the publication of my book *The Step Child*, many people have written to me and said how brave I am for speaking out. I don't think I'm brave. I spoke about it because I always knew that what had happened to me was wrong, and I truly believe that if we do something bad, one day we will be punished for it. When I was a little girl I thought I was bad because that is what I was told. However, as I grew up and realised that people liked me and that I was a good person with good values, I knew that I had to tell my story. I have had to do this no matter how shocking it has been to others, or how painful it has been for me, because being able to talk about it has relieved me of some very terrible memories and dark moments.

If memories have been stirred for you while reading this, please tell someone. Be careful though, because the person you choose will affect how you feel about your own story. Find someone whom you trust with this knowledge. You have to know that this person will be respectful of your story and guide you in the right direction, in the same way Linda has for me. If you are struggling with issues from your past I would suggest that you look for the best professional help out there. I put my past away when I left home because it was too awful to face and too terrible to talk about; and, to be perfectly honest, I just didn't think anyone would believe me anyway. But burying the past is not the right thing to do because you don't know when it is going to affect you. In the relationship I had with what I call my 'abusive' partner, I didn't see the warning signs until it was far too late.

If you take anything from this book, please let it be not to leave things too late. You owe it to yourself.

It all seems to have come full circle. By telling my story I have faced up to so much of my own life. The horrors I experienced as a little girl didn't stop when Helen Ford left my Dad, nor did they stop when I became a woman. That day, not so long ago, when I went to see Paul's new flat with him will never leave me – but I can grow stronger from it.

As we approached the basement together, I was overwhelmed by the smell: the sweet, acrid, musty smell of an old tenement. That smell was enough to transport me back to around the time I was nine, to one of the very few occasions I was allowed out by Helen. Although I wasn't involved in the games being played by the other children, I was just happy to be out in the fresh air. Sometimes Helen would do this – she'd send all of us out all day, tell us not to leave the street, and to come as soon as we were called. At those times, there would be no food and I wouldn't dare go in and ask for anything, not even the toilet. I often wondered then what she was doing and why she sometimes had this bizarre change of heart. Now I believe it may have coincided with visits from the man she was having an affair with.

The memory that came back to me that day was from the school summer holidays. As usual, I was sitting in my bed when I heard Helen shouting: 'You! Get out of that bed and get dressed! NOW!' I did as I was told, then she opened the bedroom door and gave her usual spiel about not coming back until I was called and not leaving the street. I was so delighted to be allowed out that I flew out of the door as if I had wings. I liked this occasional opportunity to get out because there was always the chance I could pick up a sweetie or something on the street, and if I went in the back greens, I could pick up stale bits of bread that had been thrown out for the birds. I was as excited as could be.

The day passed quickly as I had my imagination to rely on. Before long, I realised that I had been out all day and most of the kids had gone indoors for their tea. I was sitting outside the stairway one door down from our house, drawing with some chalk that one of the girls had left behind, when I saw him.

He was walking up the street.

I didn't know his name. I just knew he was one of the men who had often come into my room.

I was absolutely terrified and, as I looked up, he spotted me. Helen's words were still ringing in my ears and I knew that there was no way I could go into the house. I wouldn't dare. I ran into the stairway and down into the basement. It was dark and the back green door was locked as it often was, so I hid by the coal cellar door. I could hear all the noises from the flats and I could smell all the dinners being cooked. My heart was racing. Had I managed to evade him? Had he even noticed where I had gone?

I crouched down as small as I possibly could in the dark corner by the cellar door, then I heard a noise. His footsteps were coming down to the basement. As he approached the bottom of the stairs, he started calling my name softly, almost in a whisper. I could smell him – drink and fags and a sort of workman smell. God, how I hate that smell.

As he approached me, still calling 'Donna' in a quiet voice, I stood up and tried to run past him. He was quicker than me. He grabbed me and put his hand over my mouth, telling me to be very quiet. When he finally took his hand off my mouth, I tried to pull away. 'I have to go,' I said to him. 'Helen will want me home!' He knew I was lying. Helen couldn't have cared less. 'Shh!' he said. 'It's all right. Helen will be fine.'

Looking back, I can't help but go over my options – I wish I had run up the street instead of into the stairway. The man had a jacket in his hand, a sort of blue workman's jacket, and he laid it down on the basement floor. I knew then what he intended to do. I knew there was no getting away from it – or was there? Just as he laid the jacket down, we both heard one of the flat doors open above us. The man immediately pulled me towards him and put his hand over my mouth again. I heard the clip-clopping of shoes descending the stairs before they finally went out the front door. As it slammed shut, the man pushed me down roughly on top of his jacket.

It felt like there was something in his pocket. I could feel it digging into me.

I closed my eyes tight shut and tried to block out what was going to happen next. He prised my legs open and started trying to force his penis into me. It hurt so much. The smell of him was nauseating. The sounds of him grunting and that of a television in the distance were all making my head spin. I tried to think of everything I could to take away all of this, but I just lay there and let him do what he wanted as I'd done so many times before with so many men.

When he was finished he got up and, after zipping his trousers closed, he handed me a hankie from his pocket and told me to wipe myself. 'Remember our secret,' he told me as he left. As he walked up the stairs I realised I was crying – but I was bleeding too. I felt so wretched. I didn't know how long I'd been down in that basement. It seemed like hours. I just sat there, crying softly, clutching my knees and wondering – as I always did – what I had done to make me so bad and deserving of all these nasty things.

ᘒ

So, going back to that place – physically as well as emotionally – did bring the terrifying memories out yet again. I have no idea how many of these memories are still there or whether they will ever surface. All I know is that I have dealt with this one now. I have brought it out into the light, and when I visit Paul's flat in future, I shall think of the lovely garden, the bright sunny rooms and my boy's optimistic outlook on the future, not my past.

Chapter Thirty-six

THE WORLD I HAVE MADE

TIME HAS PASSED SO QUICKLY. It's February 2008 and I'm sitting here, writing this, surrounded by my children. I'm in Paul and Ayumi's flat, just a stone's throw away from the home I grew up in, so close to where all the bad things happened, where I spent my childhood days wondering whether I'd be fed or abused.

It's a wonderful contrast. Here sit my three children, laughing and happy with the security of knowing that they love each other and that I would rather die than harm a hair on their heads. As I look at Paul, Claire and Saoirse, I realise that the mantra I adopted for myself – *It's never too late to have a happy childhood* – has been a healing thing for me. Through them, I've enjoyed the wonder of childhood, of knowing what it feels like to run free and to play, to have adventures, to be excited about Santa, the Tooth Fairy, the Easter Bunny, and all the other wonderful aspects of a happy childhood that I myself could only dream of.

My two older children are now young adults. As I listen to them discussing the plans they have for their futures – Paul and Ayumi's forthcoming wedding and trip to Japan, and Claire's nursing course – I feel so very proud of my achievements. Saoirse still has all of this to come, but in the meantime she chats excitedly about our forthcoming house move and having a garden again, after such a long time living in a flat. 'We'll make a den,' she says, 'in the trees at the bottom of the garden, just for us, Mum.'

I wonder if you can understand just how much these simple words mean to me. When I was a child sitting in fear in my dark boxroom, hurting and hungry, I never ever dreamed I could be this happy.

I know that I didn't come through my childhood without physical and emotional scars, but these are things I can combat and overcome because I want to. If I hadn't gone into the dark days of my past and revealed the abuse, I fear I wouldn't be in this position now where I am able to see what I have achieved in spite of the horrors of my early years, nor would I be able to heal the damage that was done to me.

In the year 2000, I was sailing through my life – or so I thought. Life was, at least, ticking over for me. I had my children and my art but I didn't have me. I didn't know me. I felt that I was a child in an adult's body. Deep down inside me was a horror that I feared – the horror of my past. At times it didn't let me settle and I just couldn't share it with anyone because . . . where would I start?

Now I sit here, eight years on, and at last I can find the peace I have always yearned for because I have told my story. I have told it not to any one individual but to the world, and I am still accepted. I feel no shame and, finally, I am free. Through telling my story, I have righted a terrible wrong.

I never really wanted to go back into my past because I was far too scared. I knew it would be terrible. And, indeed, it has been terrible, like falling into a black pit full of demons and monsters. Despite all of this, I could always see the light, and I knew all I had to do was climb back up and out. I have beaten the demons by telling my story. They won't come back. I have no room for them in my life. I have told my story and, on the whole, that has been a rewarding, cathartic experience.

ॐ

After my first book was published, I hoped that my mother or her family would materialise. Well, Breda is still missing or doesn't want to be found, and her family doesn't want to know me. Two years have gone by since I contacted her brother and I have heard nothing. That hurt back then when all my feelings were raw, but it no longer concerns me. I am no longer sad or angry at this fact. I am ambivalent.

My mother never appeared in my life when I really needed her, when I was crying through pain and hunger. She is not the kind of mother I can respect; she is not the kind of mother I am; so I wouldn't know what to say to such a woman. And for all the things that she should have offered me – her unconditional love and protection, and being a grandmother to my children – there have been other women, magnificent caring women who have come along and offered me and my children this love and nurturing, without expecting a single thing back.

No, it isn't me who is missing out here. It's you, Breda. It is you who is missing out because you do not feel the joy of love that a grandchild can give you, nor can you rest at night knowing that you have absolutely done the right thing by your children.

I'm pulled back to the moment because the sound of my children and Ayumi laughing is so loud. So wonderfully loud!

I feel blessed.

I have so much to look forward to now that I have climbed back into the light. There's no room in my life for the past now. I can finally put it on the shelf and, if anyone ever wants to know about it, they can read it. I now know that there are important reasons for telling my story: where I had no control I now do; where there was injustice there is now justice; where I was broken I am healing; and where there was darkness and pain there is now love and light.

So I leave my past here in this book and, as I sit with my children in the very street where I suffered as a child, I am no longer haunted by the memories. It's a different world now; the one I knew is long gone. When I looked into the past at the start of this journey all I could see was the child Donna sitting cowering in the dark boxroom, but she is no longer there. She is me: the adult, the mum, the artist, the woman with the knowledge that all from now on will be safe, happy and finally free.

CONCLUSION: ME

MY NAME IS Donna Ford and I am a good person.

I am Paul's mother. I love him and he loves me.

I am Claire's mother. I love her and she loves me.

I am Saoirse's mother. I love her and she loves me.

I have many friends.

I can hug and I can trust.

I can love and I am loved.

I am an artist. I can paint and draw and create beautiful things.

I can make a home for my children and I can keep them safe and secure.

I have wonderful memories of good times and good people.

My past is something I can choose to visit or choose to keep locked away until I want to look at it.

I can let my demons go.

I can celebrate who I am, and the person I have made myself. And my future?

I have no idea – but it will be golden and warm and filled with joy.

It's never too late to have a happy childhood.

And mine has taken such a very, very long time to get here . . .

$\mathcal{S}$

Epilogue

Dear Donna

When we started the process of writing your first book together, I don't think either of us could have guessed the road we would travel. I had done some research and spoken to a few people before deciding to begin ghostwriting. The advice was pretty much universal: keep your distance; see the story as a short-term project; don't expect to make a new friend. It didn't quite work out like that, did it?

The Donna I first met was a very different woman from the one I now know. You have always been strong and capable – but that comes from a deeper place these days. It comes from knowing, absolutely, that you have a character that has been shaped by you – you haven't just done a great job with your kids; you've done a great job with yourself as well.

None of this has been easy for you, and none of it will ever be made better by a few platitudes, but what you have achieved is remarkable. I can't imagine how you have coped with some of the memories thrown up by deciding to tell your story, but I knew that I wanted this book to end on something positive, something which would be there for ever, locked inside the good memories. So, I asked all of your children to write a letter to you. I've probably just created something else to make you cry in the process!

Your legacy isn't Helen Ford or what was done to you – your legacy is three beautiful, healthy, loving human beings who adore you.

Have a wonderful life, Donna – you deserve it.

Linda xxxx

Epilogue

Dear Mum

A fighter. That's how I would probably best describe you, Mum. Despite having dealt with some of the worst things life can throw at you, you have remained strong and positive. Throughout our childhood, we weren't blessed with an awful lot of money, but you never let that affect us. In fact, we had a massively rich childhood – rich with fun and laughter and adventure; we would always find something interesting and exciting on our day trips out.

I want to tell you that you are an amazingly talented woman, both as an artist and a person. You have brilliant viewpoints and can hold a conversation with anyone on any topic. You have a very sharp mind (which is pretty annoying when I try to play you at Scrabble!) and are a massively caring person. You put your family first at every opportunity, and would much rather see us have a small luxury than have anything yourself.

I strongly believe that you have given me the best start I could have hoped for in life. You have shown me a very broad way of thinking, taught me to put others first and instilled in me the importance of considering other people's feelings, always achieved by leading by example. You have made me the person I am today.

I am not only proud to have you as my Mum; I'm proud to know you as a person.

Your son – Paul xx

Dear Mum

Or should that be Mother Teresa? I sometimes wonder whether there is a single thing in this world that you can't do! If you don't know how to do something, you'll give it your best shot . . . and in the process of trying we always have a lot of fun and laughter along the way! If I ever have something that needs to be done, I always believe you will be able to help me out. I don't know how you manage it.

I couldn't even start to explain how much you actually mean to me. Not only are you my Mum, but you're a good friend too. As with all friends, we scream and shout about petty little things, we go off stomping and shouting, but it's guaranteed that in 10 minutes we'll be the best of friends again with tears of laughter rolling down our cheeks.

Mum, it was not until I attempted to read The Step Child *that I understood a lot of things that you have done for us in our life, and why you have done them the way you have. There was one incident in particular that I read which made a lot of things fall into place. You spoke about your first ever day at school and how you were sent there, all alone, in hand-me-down tatty clothes. You stood in the playground looking at all the other children, with their parents waving them off, and you felt so alone. This is so hard to write, Mum – as I'm typing, tears are rolling down my cheeks. I can hardly bear to think that you, out of everyone in the world, had to endure what you did. When any of us had a first day at school, you made it so special. Everything we had was brand new and was laid out neatly for at least a week beforehand. You took photos of us all dressed up in our shiny new uniforms, and you stood proudly with tears in your eyes as you waved at the school gates. We knew that those were tears of love – what we didn't know was they were tears for that little girl who never experienced what we did.*

Thank you, Mum, for being you. You had the worst

possible childhood, but when you had your children, you decided that things would be different. We had the best upbringing that anyone could ask for. It was full of fun, adventure, excitement, love and togetherness. I remember once when you took us for a walk at Tiningham Woods and we got lost. You turned it into an adventure . . . let's see who can find the car first! That sums you up – eccentric – but I wouldn't change you for the world. I know that you will be there for me any second of every day.

I had to stop reading The Step Child *and I'll tell you why – it was too disturbing for me to see you that way. That may be selfish of me, but I didn't want to change the way I thought of you. How could I still come to you with every little problem knowing what had happened to you as a child? It wouldn't be fair. You are my rock, my hero. I couldn't bear for the tables to turn and for you to change from being a strong woman to someone vulnerable. It's just too hard to think of.*

I don't know how you managed to bring us up so well. You are an extraordinary person and I can only hope that I will become a woman just like you. That would be an incredible achievement. All you ever think of is everyone else – well, Mum, let's start thinking of you for a change.

Thank you once again for being you. I love you more than words can say.

Love, hugs and kisses – Clairy bumbo xxxxx

Dear Mum

I want to tell you how much I love you and how special you really are. You have done so well with everything and I am just so happy that you're not anything like your Mum, but I hope I'm like you in every way even though we look nothing like each other. I know that you sometimes get a little grumpy or a little stressed but that doesn't matter because there's no such thing as perfect. I just have one more thing to say to my special Mum – I don't know how you fit such a big heart in such a small body . . .

Love you lots, Mum!

Saoirse